BARCELONA

AUTHENTIC RECIPES CELEBRATING THE FOODS OF THE WORLD

Recipes and Text
PAUL RICHARDSON

Photographs
JASON LOWE

General Editor
CHUCK WILLIAMS

BONNIER
BOOKS

CONTENTS

INTRODUCTION

13 Culinary History

15 Contemporary Cuisine

19 Eating Out

25 Markets

27 Flavours of Barcelona and Catalonia

30 Map of Barcelona and Catalonia

BEST OF BARCELONA

34 TAPAS

39 XARCUTERIA

43 OLIVE OIL

46 SEAFOOD

50 CATALAN WINE

58 FORMATGE

62 PASTISSERIES

66 XOCOLATA

REFERENCE

185 Glossary

187 Ingredient Sources

188 Index

191 Acknowledgments and
Photography Locations

RECIPES

BERENARS I TAPAS

75 PA AMB TOMÀQUET
Tomato-rubbed Bread

76 COCA DE RECAPTE
Flatbread with Aubergines, Sweet Peppers
and Olives

79 ENTREPANS AMB FORMATGE FRESC,
ANXOVES I PEBROT
Sandwiches with Fresh Cheese,
Anchovies, and Roasted Sweet Peppers

80 PANELLETS DE PINYONS
Almond and Pine Nut Biscuits

83 PA DE FETGE
Country-style Pâté

84 EMPANADA DE PEBROTS I TONYINA
Sweet Pepper and Tuna Pie

87 VARIANTES
Spicy Marinated Olives with Pickled
Vegetables and Garlic

88 ESCABETX DE SARDINES
Fried Sardines in Vinaigrette

91 COCA DE VIDRE
Sweet Pastry with Pine Nuts

92 CROQUETES DE POLLASTRE I PERNIL
Chicken and Ham Croquettes

95 GAMBES A LA PLANXA
Griddled Prawns with Garlic
and Parsley

ENTRANTS

101 GASPATXO ANDALÚS
Gazpacho

102 ALBERGINIES FARCIDES
Stuffed Aubergines

105 TREMPÓ
Majorcan Summer Salad

106 SOPA D'ALL I VEGETALS DE PRIMAVERA
Garlic and Spring Vegetable Soup

109 XATÓ
Curly Endive Salad with Salt Cod,
Anchovies, and Olives

110 SOPA DE RAP I FARIGOLA
Thyme Soup with Monkfish Medallions

113 FAVES A LA CATALANA
Catalan-style Broad Beans

114 TRINXAT
Mashed Potatoes and Cabbage

117 CEPS AL FORN
Oven-roasted Wild Mushrooms
with Garlic and Parsley

118 ESCALIVADA
Roasted Vegetable Salad

121 CALÇOTADA
Grilled Spring Onions with Romesco Sauce

122 AMANIDA CATALANA
Catalan Salad

125 CREMA DE LLENTIES
Cream of Lentil Soup with
Garlic-Herb Croutons

126 TRUITA AMB SUC
Spinach Omelette with Tomato Sauce

129 CANELONS DE FESTA
Feast-Day Cannelloni

130 FARCELLETS DE COL
Pork and Cabbage Bundles

SEGONS PLATS

137 PAELLA PARELLADA
Shellfish and Mixed Meat Paella

138 FRICANDÓ AMB MOIXERNONS
Braised Beef with Mushrooms

141 BACALLÀ AMB SAMFAINA
Salt Cod with Aubergine, Sweet Peppers,
Onion, and Tomato

142 CALDERETA DE LLAGOSTA
Lobster Soup

145 ARRÒS AMB CROSTA
Baked Rice with Chicken, Sausages,
and Chick-peas

146 POLLASTRE ROSTIT
Roast Chicken with Garlic

149 POLLASTRE AMB GAMBES
Braised Chicken with Prawns

150 LLOM AMB PRESSECS
Pork Loin with Peaches

153 ESCUDELLA I CARN D'OLLA
Two-Course Mixed Stew of Beans,
Meat, and Vegetables

154 ÀNEC AMB PANSES I CASTANYES
Roast Duck with Raisins
and Chestnuts

157 CIVET DE PORC
Pork Stew with Picada

158 COSTELLES DE XAI A LA LLOSA
AMB OLI D'HERBES
Stone-cooked Lamb Chops
with Herb Oil

161 ORADA A LA SAL
Whole Fish Baked in Salt

162 FIDEUÀ
Vegetable and Seafood Noodles

POSTRES

169 MEL I MATÓ AMB FIGUES
Fresh Cheese and Honey with Figs

170 CREMA CATALANA
Catalan Burnt Cream

173 POSTRE DEL MÚSIC
Musician's Dessert

174 MONA DE XOCOLATA
Chocolate Truffle Cake

177 FLAÓ EIVISSENC
Ibiza Goat Cheese Tart with Mint

178 PA DE PESSIC AMB AVELLANES
I REGALESSIA
Hazelnut Cake with Liquorice

181 GRANISSAT DE CAVA
"Liquid" Granita of Sparkling Wine

182 FLAM
Crème Caramel

INTRODUCTION

Situated on the Mediterranean coast, in the shadow of the Pyrenees, Barcelona is a bustling city with more than two thousand years of history. In the past two decades, it has re-invented itself as a vibrant cultural capital, making its mark in architecture, art, design, sport – and, of course, excellent food.

CULINARY HISTORY

Catalonia and its capital, Barcelona, have a long and fascinating culinary history, with moments of glittering fame and long periods of obscurity. In fact, of all of Spain's regional cuisines, it may have the deepest historical roots. Like most southern European culinary traditions, from Provence to Turkey, Catalan cuisine has its origins in the great civilisations that once ruled the Mediterranean – most obviously the Romans, who brought the olive; the Greeks, who brought the grapevine; and the Arabs, who brought sugar cane, rice, and aubergines. These raw materials flourished and are the basis of thriving industries today, including olive oil production and viticulture. When combined with the abundance of fish and shellfish from the Mediterranean and salt-cured hams and artisanal cheeses from the Pyrenees, it is easy to understand why Catalonia bears the marks of one of Europe's richest cuisines.

The first golden age of Catalan cuisine occurred in the Middle Ages. During the thirteenth and fourteenth centuries, the gastronomy of Catalonia and its capital,

Barcelona, was famous throughout Europe. Classic Catalan dishes such as *menjar blanc* (almond-milk pudding) were often prepared at the courts of Naples and Rome, and in the mid-1400s, the great Italian food writer and historian Bartolomeo Sacchi (Platina of Cremona) declared Catalan cooks to be the finest in the world.

Around the same time, some of the first books about food printed in Europe were being written by Catalan authors, among them the famous *Llibre de Sent Sovi,* a collection of recipes probably produced at the end of the twelfth century. The *Regiment de Sanitat,* published in 1307, a treatise on health and nutrition, contains a wealth of wisdom that is still true today, such as the suggestion to chew food slowly and calmly, to the accompaniment of "soft music". And finally, one of the greatest cookery books of all time, *Llibre del Coch,* was first published in Barcelona around 1520. Written in Catalan by Ruperto de Nola, chef to the Spanish King Fernando I of Naples, this cookery book contains recipes drawn from Italian, Arabic, Provençal and Catalan sources.

Even the two principal signifiers of Catalan food today come from the medieval era. One is the taste for exotic spices and for curious combinations of savoury and sweet, as found in dishes such as duck with pears and apples stuffed with meat. The other is the *picada,* a thickening agent made by pounding together nuts and herbs in a mortar with a pestle. The resulting mixture is usually stirred into the recipe in its final cooking stage, contributing an added refinement to the flavour and texture of the finished dish.

Medieval Barcelona was famous not only for the quality of its cuisine but also for the quantity. Francesc Eiximenis (1327–1409), who taught in the great academic centres of medieval Europe, wrote, "[Barcelona] is gifted with great reason and peopled with notable folk of great weight and well nourished".

In the years following this age of splendour, however, Catalan cuisine fell into gradual decline when the region was annexed by nearby Castile in the early eighteenth century. A period ensued in which the local culture was marginalised. Finally, in the early nineteenth century, with the rise of the bourgeoisie and the incipient power of Barcelona as an economic and industrial capital, Catalonia began to assume some of its old importance. The year 1840 saw the publication of a guidebook to the city's inns and restaurants. (The famous Set Portes restaurant, located in Barcelona's waterfront neighbourhood, Barceloneta, opened not long after and is still operating today.) During the latter part of the nineteenth century, Barcelona witnessed an influx of Italian restaurateurs, who influenced the cuisine and helped make pasta dishes, like *canelons* (cannelloni) and *macarrons* (macaroni), now regular items on many restaurant menus.

While the Spanish Civil War was also a bleak time for Catalonia, the postwar period was perhaps even more so. Nationalistic feeling was brutally suppressed, and the speaking, writing, and teaching of the Catalan language were prohibited. The culinary life of the region might have been richer if there had been more food to go around. Many

Barcelonans have grim memories of the endless *escudella* (mixed meat and vegetable stew eaten with rice or pasta), the lack of culinary variety, the preponderance of salt cod and reliance on pork fat for frying.

With the arrival of democracy in the region in 1975 and the new freedoms that accompanied it, Catalan cooking underwent a revival. Josep Mercader, chef at the Hotel Empordà in Figueres, came to prominence by virtue of his elegant take on the traditional cooking of the region; his legacy lives on under the direction and able hands of his successor, Jaume Subirós. At the Big Rock restaurant outside Platja d'Aro, Carles Camós began the work of rescuing traditional Catalan food from the doldrums into which it had sunk during the post-Civil War era. Inspired by these culinary revivalists, a roster of talented young chefs began to emerge, notably Santi Santamaria, Carme Ruscalleda, Carles Gaig, and Joan Roca. Traditional Catalan dishes were rediscovered and even re-invented, while foreign flavours and new techniques were

incorporated as never before. Ferran Adrià, one of the most exciting chefs working anywhere in the world, and his restaurant El Bulli shot to fame (and to three Michelin stars) as the creator of a whole new attitude to food.

With Adrià at the helm, Catalan cuisine is moving into a second golden age. At the same time, care is being taken to avoid the loss of the traditional virtues of the cuisine in a swirl of foams and deconstructions. Pepa Aymamí and her Institut de la Cuina Catalana are working to ensure the survival of such classic Catalan dishes as *fricandó* (meat stew) and *rossejat* (rice or pasta baked in fish broth) in a world that has almost forgotten them. The institute is attempting to give Catalan cuisine protected status under UNESCO's World Heritage. Food writers such as Jaume Fàbrega and Pep Palau, as well as magazines such as *Descobrir Cuina,* are also making vital contributions towards preserving the culinary legacy of the past.

They have their work cut out for them, because the region's food is continually evolving. In recent years, Barcelona has transformed itself into a multicultural capital, and the city's eating habits have changed with it. Where once you could barely find a Chinese restaurant, now there are not only Chinese, but Indian, Moroccan, Mexican, Turkish, and Japanese as well. Even macrobiotic and vegetarian kitchens are popular. Indeed, the city's restaurant scene has never been so vibrant, and today Catalan cuisine is recognised as one of the most dynamic in the world.

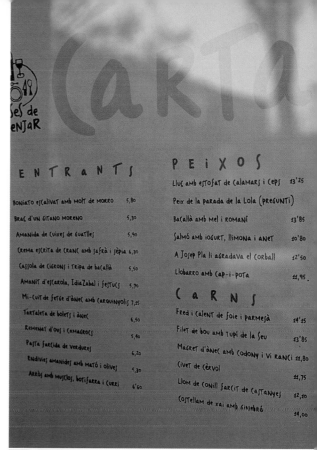

CONTEMPORARY CUISINE

Barcelona's economy has boomed in the years since its triumphant hosting of the 1992 Olympics, and its food scene has blossomed along with it. Traditional cuisine is still the city's mainstay, but new trends and international influences are revitalising the landscape, making Barcelona a culinary hot spot.

Defining Catalan cuisine is not easy. But then, defining Catalonia is not easy, either. It is a region with its own language and a strong sense of place and identity. At the same time, it is a part of the Spanish state, co-existing more or less harmoniously with Andalusia, Galicia, Navarre, and all of the other so-called autonomous communities that make up Spain.

The definition is further complicated by the *països catalans,* satellite regions of Catalan influence that sprang from the same historical roots yet have no political connection with Catalonia itself. These "Catalan lands" consist of the region of Valencia, farther south down the coast of the Mediterranean; the Balearic Islands of Majorca, Minorca, Ibiza, and Formentera; an area known as French Catalonia, part of France extending north of the Spanish border; and the north-west corner of Sardinia in Italy.

As with geography, so with gastronomy. Catalonia is both separate from the rest of Spain and united with it by a great deal of commonality. In terms of cuisine, it is impossible to separate out a pure, unadulterated Catalan cuisine from the influences that surround it, hence the presence in this book of recipes for flan, gazpacho, and *croquetas*.

That said, it is the Catalans, perhaps along with the Basques, who possess the most sophisticated gastronomic life of any Spanish region. One factor is the sheer number of dishes that make up the repertoire of *la cuina catalana* – more than 150, according to some estimates. Another is the variety. Almost every *comarca* (county) of Catalonia, indeed almost every village, has something food-related that it claims as its own, whether it is a special vegetable variety, such as peas in the Maresme, turnips in the Empordà, or potatoes in Osona; a food-based fiesta like the *xatonada* of Sitges (see page 109); or a complex archaic dish like *El Niu,* from Palafrugell on the Costa Brava.

Catalans love their food and are serious about it, but not in a long-faced, solemn manner. *La cuina catalana* is food for families, for friends, and for communities. In its purest form, the cuisine of Catalonia is not naturally suited to the restaurant environment, and when it appears on the menus of famous Catalan chefs such as Santi Santamaria and Carme Ruscalleda, it is usually presented in a simplified and modernised form. It is essentially a rural and working-class tradition, the heritage of fishermen and peasant farmers.

But above all else, Catalan cooking is Mediterranean. The presence of the sea is probably the single most important influence on the way people eat in this part of the world. Catalonia has more than two hundred miles (325 km) of coastline, so it comes as no surprise that fish and shellfish are pillars of the local diet. Fresh fish is normally grilled (the favourite cooking technique), baked, or combined with potatoes and stock in an *all cremat, suquet, romesco, sarsuela,* or one of

the dozen or so other Catalan variants of fish stew. Prawns and other crustaceans are of superb quality, particularly the famous *gambes de Palamós.* Cured and preserved fish plays an important role; the salt anchovies of the coastal town L'Escala are famous throughout Spain. Salt cod is also extremely popular and forms the basis for some of Catalonia's most famous dishes, notably *xató* (curly endive salad with salt cod; page 109), *esqueixada* (shredded salt cod salad; page 36), and *bacallà a la llauna* (baked salt cod with garlic and pimentón (smoked paprika).

Gastronomically and geographically speaking, the region is divided into rivers, fertile plains, deserts, and soaring mountains. From the inland districts come excellent meat and dairy products, fruit, vegetables, and snails. From the mountains come game and trout from the Pyrenean rivers. Rice from the Ebro Delta in the south of the region is used in dishes such as *arròs negre* (black rice), *arròs a banda* (rice with fish stock), and various local versions of paella.

Any world cuisine worthy of consideration gives the greatest respect to vegetables, and *la cuina catalana* is no exception. The sensational displays at markets such as Barcelona's La Boqueria are powerful evidence that the quality is high. Some of the best Catalan dishes are based on vegetables: Broad beans for *faves a la catalana* (page 113), spinach with raisins and pine nuts, and cabbage and potatoes for *trinxat* (page 114). Wild mushrooms are a national obsession, and the forests teem with mushroom hunters during the autumn months. Dried pulses such as lentils, beans, and chick-peas form the basis for rib-sticking soup-stews like the famous *escudella i carn d'olla* (page 153).

Despite the variety in Catalan cuisine, some generalisations can be made. Catalan eaters by and large seem to enjoy the mixture of sweet and sour more than any other people in Western Europe – arguably a legacy of the medieval glory days of *la cuina catalana*. (A propensity for adding spices, particularly cinnamon, to meat dishes is surely a medieval

throwback, too.) They adore the flavour and texture of nuts, which are pounded with herbs as part of the famous *picada* and used as a thickener for braised and baked dishes. They have a notable sweet tooth, so a good *pastisseria,* or patisserie, in Catalonia will never be short of clientele.

Both Catalans and their food are by nature festive and celebratory. Any excuse will do to throw a party based around one of their favourite dishes, whether it be the *truita amb suc,* a spinach omelette with tomato sauce (page 126) from the Priorat, or the *cassola de tros,* a monumental stew of rabbit, snails, and mixed vegetables, each of which has its corresponding *festa.* Taking part in *la calçotada,* the feast of a

special type of grilled spring onions called *calçots,* dunked in romesco sauce, is an intensely Catalan experience in itself (see page 121).

And at the heart of it all, where the various cross-currents of Catalan cuisine meet and mingle, is the city of Barcelona. If the Catalan capital has not been famous for its food in the past, that may be only because Gaudí, the Olympics, the Barcelona football club, and the reputation of the city as a world design mecca have stolen its thunder as a gastronomic capital. The situation is rapidly changing, however, as culinary observers worldwide realise that, in terms of both traditional and contemporary cooking, Barcelona represents a formidable force.

EATING OUT

Until recently, Barcelona was a city in which meals were often eaten at home and cooked in a traditional style. Nowadays, the reverse is true. This is a city in love with eating out. Restaurants of all types, sizes and price levels abound in every neighbourhood. If variety is the spice of life, Barcelona is a hot prospect indeed.

In a part of the world where life, or much of its social activity, plays out *al carrer* – "in the street" – the restaurant constitutes a vitally important part of the local culture. It is seen as a neutral space, free from the tedious routines of home and work, where the only imperatives are sensuous enjoyment and the pleasure of human interaction.

As a restaurant town, Barcelona may not be on the A list with Paris or New York, but it is certainly riding at the top of the B list. The choice and variety are enormous, and it is

possible to eat well on any budget. At the lower end of the price scale are the *casas de comida,* simple eating-houses where a full three-course meal, including wine and coffee, can be had for very little money. At the upper end of the scale, the top chefs of Barcelona cuisine work their magic for those who can afford it at restaurants of international renown such as Neichel, Jean Luc Figueras, Gaig, Drolma, and Talaia-Mar.

In between these extremes are the neighbourhood restaurants, the chic,

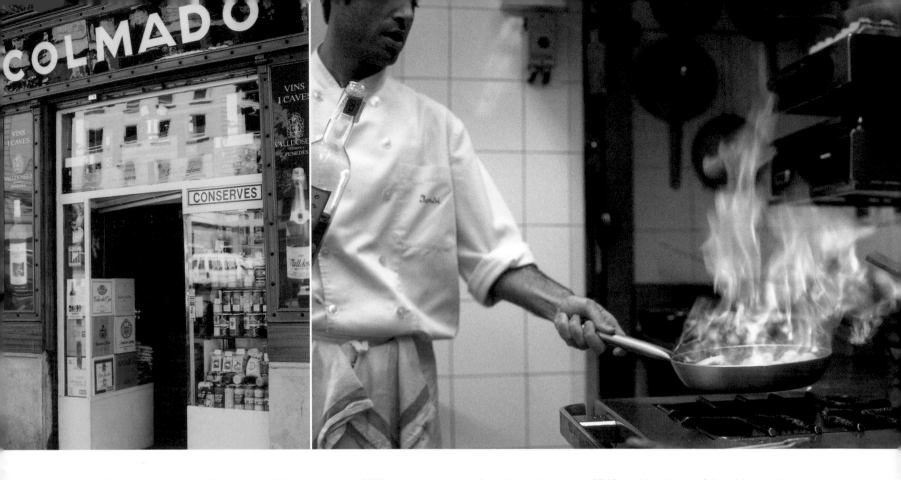

so-called *restaurants de disseny* – the fish restaurants, the *asadores* (grill rooms), and the beachside *chiringuitos* – where the style of the place has as much to say as the food on your plate. Then there are the ethnic restaurants, a sector that has blossomed marvellously in recent years, with the foods of Japan, China, Pakistan, Turkey, Lebanon, and Morocco all well-represented. Also prominent are restaurants serving dishes from other regions of Spain, notably Galicia, Andalusia, and the Basque country, fare from closer to home but still vaguely exotic, even to locals.

Ironically, although foreign and fusion cuisines fill the culinary limelight – testimony to Barcelona's open-mindedness – authentic Catalan cooking, the kind of food the region's grandmothers used to make, seems under-represented in Barcelona. Luckily, the city has a handful of restaurants that have always served real Catalan food and show no signs of letting it fade into the shadows. Set Portes, founded in 1836 and still serving *paella Parellada* (rice with seafood and mixed meat;

page 137) and *canelons de festa* (baked cannelloni; page 129) to appreciative hordes of tourists and locals alike, is the most famous of the lot. Another local favourite is Gargantua i Pantagruel, a sleekly designed restaurant featuring the specialities of Lleida and the surrounding region – dishes such as *cargols a la llauna* (baked snails) and *bacallà* (salt cod) with honey. Estimable traditional preparations are featured at Senyor Parellada, the flagship of Ramón Parellada's small chain of restored lodging houses. Cal Isidre, run for two decades by Isidre Gironés, his wife Montse, and daughter Núria, is a restaurant that understands perhaps best of all how to coax the glories of classic Catalan cuisine into the modern world. This is one of the few eateries in Barcelona where one can enjoy a perfectly presented *bacallà a la llauna* (oven-roasted salt cod) or a scrumptious *suquet* (stew) of monkfish.

Three of the longest-running *casas de comida* in town are Cal Estevet, Can Lluis, and Can Culleretes (the last was founded in

1740, making it one of the oldest restaurants in the world), all serving hearty meals with wine at modest prices. El Celler Nou represents a slightly more upmarket option, though it is thoroughly Catalan in its tavern-like decoration and appealingly rustic cooking.

For a taste of the classic Spanish *chiringuito,* the kind of beachside restaurant where you shake off the sand from your feet as you come through the door, try the family-run Xiringuito Escribà on Bogatell beach (just south of the Olympic village) owned by the Escribà brothers (see Pastisseries, page 65). With a menu devised by Carles Abellán of the elegant Comerç 24 and desserts from the Escribà family, the food is a cut above the average *chiringuito,* and there is nowhere better in Barcelona to see, smell and hear the sea as you feast on local seafood.

Away from the city's sometimes frenzied jostling for fashionability, both food and life tend to stick closer to the land. Out in the Catalan countryside, a new generation is looking again at its culinary roots while

smoothly assimilating the influence of modernist fashions. In the hills around the town of Vic, a collective of young chefs calling itself Osona Cuina is doing a great job of promoting the range of local ingredients, including wild mushrooms and truffles, potatoes, and game. The collective, along with other individuals in Vic, such as Nando Jubany and Jordi Parramón, is today's equivalent of the generation of far-sighted chefs who revolutionised Catalan cooking in the 1980s. Further off the beaten path in the Catalonian town of Olot, another champion of the new Spanish cuisine has arisen at Les Cols, a restaurant that practically brings the farmyard to the table.

The work of the new Catalan chefs in Barcelona encompasses a wide range of different styles, from the sophisticated luxury of Xavier Pellicer at Abac and Fermi Puig at Drolma to the streetwise swagger of places like Ot, Hisop, Sauc, and Biblioteca. The last few years have seen a mania for fusion food, mixing and matching Asian ingredients with Mediterranean techniques (or vice versa). Although this tendency is fast approaching saturation point, there is still excitement to be found in the trendy, design-driven restaurants of neighbourhoods like the Born and Raval. Today, the DJ restaurant, in which a person in headphones spins dance music while you try to make yourself heard across the table, is very much in vogue in Barcelona (Salsitas, Oven, Salero, and Fuse are good examples), as are restaurants conceived as lounges, where diners can linger into the early hours.

While women may have long been the stalwarts of Catalan home cooking, the star chefs of haute cuisine have been men. At last, however, women's contributions to the culinary scene are being recognised, and some of the most important chefs in Catalonia are female. Paquita and Lolita Reixach, who began running a "pull-up for carmen" fifty years ago, are now acclaimed for their magnificent country cooking at one of the country's best restaurants, the Hispania in Arenys de Mar.

A little farther along the coast, in Sant Pol de Mar, is another culinary wizard, Carme Ruscalleda, perhaps the most brilliant of all Catalonia's cooks, male or female, and certainly among the world's outstanding women chefs. Ruscalleda is a culinary powerhouse whose capacity for work is as unlimited as her imagination. Her cooking might be described as a contemporary and intensely personal take on the Catalan food of her childhood, a reflection of the treasure trove of local produce ranging from fish and shellfish to vegetables and fruit.

As you might expect from a community with a long Mediterranean coastline, Catalonia has an enormous appetite for the local catch. Seafood restaurants form a vital and important category within the food scene, especially in the towns and cities of the Mediterranean seaboard. In Barcelona itself, fish cooking in general is of high quality, but it is truly exceptional in the Barceloneta, a former fishing district just below the Barri Gòtic. The harbour front of the Port Vell (old port) is a

long strip of restaurants, nearly all of which specialise in *la cuina marinera* – "seafood cookery". The typical menu in this part of the city centres on fish *a la planxa* (seared on a griddle; *a la placha* in Spanish). It is then incorporated into mixed rice dishes such as *arròs a banda* (cooked in fish stock) or paella, or served with pasta (*fideuà*). Certain dishes at El Suquet de l'Almirall are famous in Barcelona: the crisp *calamares a la romana* (line-caught squid, battered and fried in olive oil), for example, are reputed to be the best in the city. Els Pescadors, in the city's once little-visited, but increasingly popular Poble Nou district, is a long-running operation that hits all the right notes: a lovely old dining-room with its original whitewashed walls and marble tables and a menu that goes beyond the usual seafood repertoire into *fricandó de rap* (monkfish stew) and *arròs cremós de gambes amb formatge fumat* (creamy rice with prawns and smoked goat's cheese).

MARKETS

All over the world, supermarkets are replacing the traditional food markets which are becoming a thing of the past. Not so in Barcelona. The city's neighbourhood markets are very much alive, and none more so than the bustling Mercat de Sant Josep, known as La Boqueria, one of the best places to shop for seasonal foods.

People visiting Barcelona for the first time are often surprised to discover that, along with the renowned Gaudí buildings and the Picasso Museum, the city also possesses one of the world's greatest food markets. The Mercat de Sant Josep, better known as La Boqueria, is one of about forty covered food markets in the capital, and the most spectacular. Others worth a look are the Mercat de Sant Antoni, with its grand Parisian-style ironwork building, and the charming Mercat de Gràcia, in the Gràcia neighbourhood. Oddly, Barcelona does not have many street markets, though there is one notable exception: the Plaça del Pi. Held on the first Saturday and Sunday of every month, this market offers artisanal cheeses, chocolate, herbs, honey, bread and cakes, and other locally made products.

La Boqueria was once the site of a convent of Carmelite monks, until the structure burned down in 1835 and a fine new market was established in its place. In 1914, it was given a roof and a decorative stained-glass *modernista* entrance leading directly off the Ramblas, Barcelona's bustling main thoroughfare. It is a cause for celebration that this huge and vibrant market – the largest in Spain at about twenty thousand square feet (6,000 sq m) – is still alive and kicking at the heart of the city centre and hasn't been hauled out to the suburbs to make way for ritzy shops and luxury flats. For the three hundred families who make their living here, La Boqueria is just like a village, complete with gossip, friendships, and village personalities, such as Juanito at the Bar

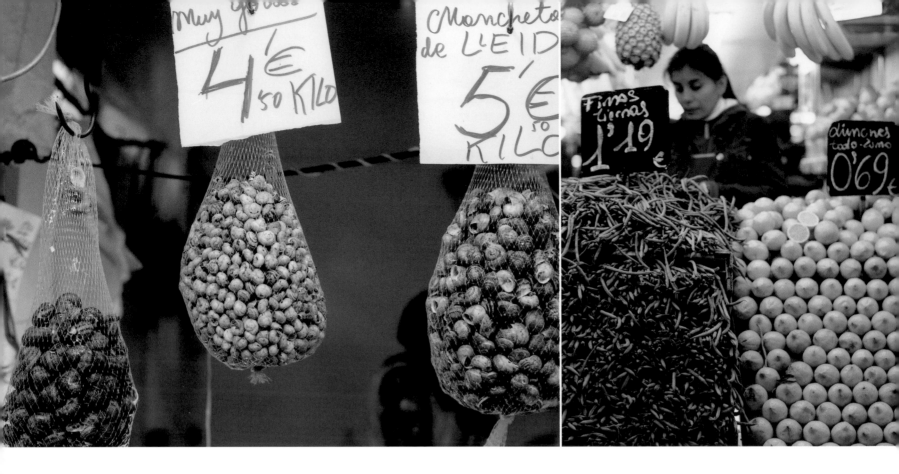

Pinotxo, fruiterer Eduard Soley, and Marta at the fish stall Peixos Marta.

La Boqueria represents all that is best in Catalan ingredients (though not always at the best possible prices). Most of the top-quality local produce finds its way to this market. In the fish section, Marisc Genaro's stall is especially worth a visit for its displays of shellfish. Salted and cured fish, such as *bacallà,* cured tuna roe, and salt herring are the order of the day at Especialitats Salaons. No fewer than seventy-two fruit and vegetable stalls cover the entire range of Catalan and Spanish produce, and exotic fruits, even such eccentricities as starfruit (carambola) and durian, are increasingly easy to find, too. For hams and charcuterie, the best source is generally thought to be Cansaladeria Mateo López, where maestro Mateo specialises in Iberian hams and other fine pork products, many from beyond the borders of Catalonia, excellent in their own right.

All tastes are catered to at La Boqueria. If it's snails you want, the place to go is a tiny, nameless stall on the corner of the Carrer Sagres. A scrawled notice advertises *auténtics cargols de Lleida* – "genuine snails from the town of Lleida" – in sizes ranging from big, fat Vinyals to the smaller Monxeta and Bobe varieties. If your taste runs to game, Salvador Capdevila will sell you just about anything your heart desires, from venison, wild boar, and hare to partridge and wild duck.

The bars of La Boqueria are a vital element of the market's broader function. Hearty *esmorzars de forquilla* (simply prepared "fork" breakfasts) featuring such dishes as braised pig's trotters and salt cod with beans are served up for the market workers at a time of the morning when most of us are just beginning to contemplate our first cup of coffee. The Bar Pinotxo, near the entrance, is perhaps the market's most famous tapas bar and its owner, Juanito, its best-known personality. While he presides out front, chatting with customers, preparing coffee or pouring drinks, the younger generation cooks up dozens of orders at the back of the tiny kitchen, making good use of the day's freshest produce. Among other delights, Bar Pinotxo makes one of the finest *pa amb tomàquet* (tomato-rubbed bread; page 75) in Barcelona. El Quim de la Boqueria in the heart of the market is a nice place to take the weight off your feet and try a little tapa, a medium-sized *ración,* a *bocadillo* (sandwich), or a full-scale meal. Proprietor Quim is busy at the stove from eight in the morning; later in the day, he composes a brilliant menu reflecting his morning's adventures around the stalls. Never has "market cooking" been more literally that.

Before you leave, don't miss the simple stalls set up outside the market by women who bring in their produce from the *masies* (rural farmhouses). These stalls aren't officially part of the market, but the quality is just as good. Here you will often see Pakistani and Moroccan immigrants doing their shopping. Clearly they know a good thing when they see it – as do all the clients of the beautiful La Boqueria.

FLAVOURS OF BARCELONA AND CATALONIA

Eating in Barcelona is a complex interplay of origins, influences and traditions. As you travel through the city's neighbourhoods, keep your eyes open and your palate attuned to the different flavours offered at each stop. The same is true in the surrounding regions, where the cuisines are united by a common history.

Barri Gòtic

Some of Barcelona's prime food hot spots are found in the tourist-ridden streets of the medieval old town known as Barri Gòtic. The dominant categories here are old-fashioned Catalan restaurants with historical roots – places like Can Culleretes (established in 1740) and Agut (established in 1924) – and ancient taverns perfect for a glass of wine and a bite to eat. Look for the superlative Lls Quatre Gats, Ll Xampanyet, or Ll Pintor. Formatgeria La Seu, a shop specialising in Spanish farmhouse cheeses, is a gem, and around the corner, El Mesón del Café serves what is perhaps Barcelona's best cup of coffee. Shunka, close to the cathedral, is a superb Japanese restaurant frequented by the likes of renowned chef Ferran Adrià.

Born

Clustered around the former produce market of Born, this neighbourhood (the southern end of which is known as La Ribera) is Barcelona's fashion zone. It is also the heartland of trendy restaurants patronised by trendy people, featuring chefs creating wild fusion cuisine with an emphasis on Asian Flavours. Visit Nao Colon, Salero, Arrel del Born, or Café Kafka for some of the best experiences of this kind.

Amid the designer frippery characterising this neighbourhood is some real creative excellence. Check out the inventive tapas at Santa Maria, Estrella de Plata, Cal Pep or Comerç 24, Carles Abellán's highly fashionable post-modern tapas salon. La Vinya del Senyor is one of the city's best wine bars, and Abac is possibly its finest restaurant.

Raval

Raval is a melting pot of immigrants from Africa, Asia, South America, and eastern Europe. Once the Barrio Chino, or Chinatown, this neighbourhood now hums with Asian supermarkets, hallal butchers, and designer delis – not to mention La Boqueria market (page 25). Predominant flavours are spicy and exotic, reflecting the influx of Pakistanis and Moroccans into the barrio. The Shalimar on Carrer Carme was Barcelona's first Pakistani restaurant and still ranks as one of the best. Meanwhile, the bohemian invasion of Raval has spawned a new wave of designer "lounges", combining electronic music with chic design and audacious fusion food.

Barceloneta

As befits this former fishing district down by the sea, the Barceloneta is a great destination for seafood. Fish lovers prowl the narrow streets of this wonderfully atmospheric barrio in search of classic fish stews like *suquet* and *sarsuela,* as well as other Catalan fish dishes. Start off with tapas at Cova Fumada, then move on to Cheriff, reputed to serve Barcelona's best paella, or to Restaurant

Barceloneta for *arròs negre* (black rice) and staggering plates of shellfish. Can Majó, run by the Suárez family for the last thirty years, is reliably high quality and has a lovely open-air *terraza*. Can Solé, a famous seafood restaurant, still has its original one-hundred-year-old decor. Ricart, the fish shop just around the corner, was founded in 1939.

L'Eixample

L'Eixample is the nerve centre of bourgeois Barcelona. Passeig de Gràcia, a lively avenue cutting through the neighbourhood, is where you will find three famous buildings by the excentric architect Antoni Gaudí. L'Eixample is also home to many of the city's grandest restaurants. Hotel restaurants come into their own here: at the top are Drolma in the Hotel Majestic and East 47 at Hotel Claris. This elegant neighbourhood tends towards a more progressive take on contemporary cuisine; Sauc and Hisop are two restaurants to watch for new trends. Keep an eye out for old *colmados,* or general stores, that are now enjoying a new lease on life as luxury delis. The best include Mantequeria Ravell, Murrià, and Quílez, which have superb selections of local cheeses, cured meat, sausages, and an excellent selection of wines. Finally, be sure to visit the barrio's two state-of-the-art chocolate makers, Xocoa and Sampaka.

Gràcia

This former working-class district has a quiet bohemian charm and some intriguing food offerings. Lebanese, Turkish, Greek, and Balkan foods are conspicuous; there are few better places in Barcelona to get a good souvlaki. Another culinary treat is the barrio's ethnic pastries, which range from bagels to Argentinian empanadas to the Arab pastries at Principe. The bread at Fleca Fortino rates among the best in Barcelona. Mercat de Llibertat, housed in a charming art nouveau building, functions as the local food market and is better than central markets you find in most cities. This is also the location of Ot, one of Barcelona's most exciting new restaurants.

Girona, Empordà, and Costa Brava

This northern coastal area of Catalonia has a unique gastronomic tradition of its own – *mar i muntanya,* the mixing of seafood with meat. The *platillos* of the Empordà are rich, rustic combinations of offal, snails, and game. At its best, the fish and seafood of the Costa Brava are peerless. The *suquet,* a simple Catalan stew of fish and potatoes, is superb, and don't miss the famous prawns from the coastal towns of Palamós and Roses. Some of the best restaurants in Catalonia are found in this region. The kitchen at Hotel Empordà was one of the progenitors of the new Catalan cuisine and is still going strong under chef Jaume Subirós. In Girona, you will find Celler de Can Roca, one of the very best restaurants in Spain, and farther up the Costa Brava, in the town of Roses, is a local restaurant that is known around the world: El Bulli.

Lleida

Lleida is one of Spain's great fruit-growing regions. The apples, pears, and plums are famous, as are the vegetables grown on the well-watered plains around it. Les Garrigues, an important olive oil producing region in Lleida, makes a golden yellow, fruity oil of superb quality. Catalan cuisine also relies on another major product of this area – almonds, pistachios, and other nuts. The southern end of the region has a huge appetite for snails, which are typically cooked *a la llauna* ("on the tin", i.e., baked in the oven) or *a la gormanda* (with onion, ham, garlic, and chilli peppers). Aplec del Cargol is Lleida's great festival for snail-lovers. The northern part of Lleida includes the high Pyrenees, which has its own culinary contributions, in the form of fine goat's and sheep's milk cheeses and French-influenced dishes such as *sopa de ceba* (onion soup).

Tarragona

Tarragona constitutes the southernmost part of Catalonia proper, half-way between Barcelona and the Catalan-speaking lands of Valencia and Alicante. The town of Valls, and by extension the whole region, is best known gastronomically for its massive consumption of *calçots* (grilled spring onions, page 121). Tarragona is also the home of romesco, the fish stew and the sauce of the same name, both of which include peanuts – and of the salad *xató*. Rice from the Ebro Delta is produced in small quantities, but it is of exceptional quality. Honey from the fragrant hills of Port de Beseit is said to be the best in Catalonia. Inland lies the mountainous region in which some of Spain's finest red wines are made. Monsant, Priorat and Tarragona are three highly respected local growing areas.

Països Catalans

The *països catalans* extend beyond the official boundaries of Catalonia and include the "autonomous community" of Valencia, the four Balearic islands (Majorca, Minorca, Ibiza, and Formentera), the independent country of Andorra, high in the Pyrenees, and the north-west corner of Sardinia.

Valencia is synonymous with one of the best loved dishes in the Spanish repertoire, *paella valenciana*. In fact, rice is the basis for many Valencian dishes, including *arròs a banda* (rice with fish stock), *arròs al forn* (baked rice), and the famous *arròs amb crosta* of Elche (baked rice with an egg crust; page 145). Valencia is also known for its bounty of fresh fruit and vegetables – the region is Europe's leading producer of oranges – and the city's beautiful Mercat Central is second only to Barcelona's La Boqueria in size and excellence. From the southern part of the region, whose capital is Alicante, comes *turron* (almond nougat), a candy enjoyed at Christmas all over Spain and beyond.

The four islands of the Balearics share many ingredients and dishes, but each is fiercely proud of its own culinary tradition. Seafood naturally forms a major part of the island diet, followed by *sobrassada,* a minced pork sausage cured with chilli pepper. Vegetables, fruit, and nuts, especially almonds, also play an important role.

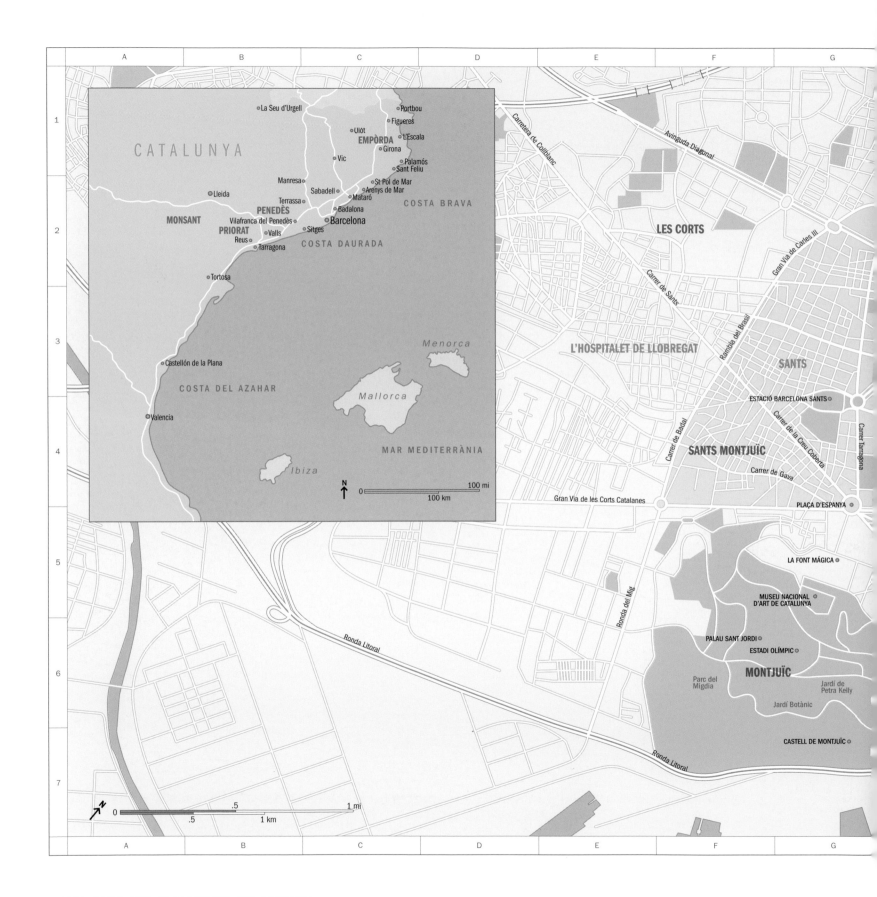

CATALUNYA

La Seu d'Urgell
Portbou
Figueres
Ulòt
L'Escala
EMPÒRDA
Girona
Vic
Palamós
Sant Feliu
Manresa
St Pol de Mar
Sabadell
Arenys de Mar
Lleida
Mataró
Terrassa
Badalona
PENEDÈS
Barcelona
MONSANT
Vilafranca del Penedès
COSTA BRAVA
PRIORAT
Valls
Sitges
Reus
COSTA DAURADA
Tarragona
Tortosa
Menorca
Castellón de la Plana
Mallorca
COSTA DEL AZAHAR
Valencia
MAR MEDITERRÀNIA
Ibiza

N
0   100 mi
0   100 km

Carretera de Collblanc
Avinguda Diagonal
LES CORTS
Gran Via de Carles III
Carrer de Sants
L'HOSPITALET DE LLOBREGAT
Rambla del Brasil
SANTS
ESTACIÓ BARCELONA SANTS
Carrer de la Creu Coberta
Carrer Tarragona
SANTS MONTJUÏC
Carrer de Badal
Carrer de Gava
Gran Via de les Cortes Catalanes
PLAÇA D'ESPANYA
LA FONT MÀGICA
MUSEU NACIONAL
D'ART DE CATALUNYA
Ronda del Mig
PALAU SANT JORDI
ESTADI OLÍMPIC
MONTJUÏC
Ronda Litoral
Parc del
Migdia
Jardí de
Petra Kelly
Jardí Botànic
CASTELL DE MONTJUÏC
Ronda Litoral

N
0   .5   1 mi
0   .5   1 km

Best of **BARCELONA**

Whichever venue you choose for taking an aperitif in Barcelona, you will find something there to eat with it: a plate of *ibérico* ham, a slice of Manchego cheese, toasted bread rubbed with tomato and drizzled with olive oil *(pa amb tomàquet),* or a bowl of spicy olives.

TAPAS

Catalonia has a complex relationship with the rest of Spain, and this is as true of its eating – and snacking – habits as anything else. A wide variety of tapas, little dishes eaten with drinks, are served all over Spain, including Catalonia. But the tapas habit still belongs more to the non-Catalans in Catalonia than to the Catalans themselves. When the locals snack, they do it differently. *Raciones* (medium-sized servings) of sliced sausage and hams; *entrepans* stuffed with fresh cheese and anchovies (page 79); bowls of olives and nuts; or tomato-rubbed bread (page 75) are local alternatives to the typical Spanish repertoire of tapas. That said, you can find excellent tapas in Barcelona. Cal Pep and Bar Pinotxo (in La Boqueria market) are arguably the two best tapas outposts in town and are deservedly popular with locals.

Other Spanish regional traditions have made their mark on Catalan eating habits as well. Basque-style bars have cropped up around Barcelona, with trays of *pintxos* (snacks) on the bar to be eaten at will and paid for later. The favourite drinks are dry red Rioja wine or cider, served in the flat-bottomed glasses typical of the Basque country. Galicians were probably the first immigrants to establish a community in Barcelona, and many of their bars offer such regional small dishes as *pulpo a feira* (octopus with paprika and olive oil) and tuna-stuffed empanadas. Meanwhile, updated *cerveserias* – stylish "beer halls" like the Ciudad Condal – cheerfully mix and match local food and drink traditions with whatever takes their fancy.

Some of the best tapas in town are tangy snacks composed of cured or pickled foods.

At Quimet i Quimet, a one-room bodega in Poble Sec, the selection, or *surtido,* is a miniature feast made up daily on the spot from such items as wild mushrooms in oil, tuna *escabetx,* pickled baby onions, or slices of *mojama* (cured tuna roe). Xampanyet, a few doors down from the Picasso Museum, also specialises in pickles – don't miss the crunchy, sweet, whole garlic cloves.

Finally, there is the *tapa de autor*. Chefs such as Carles Abellán, at superchic Comerç 24; Paco Guzmán, presiding at Santa Maria across the street; and Didac López, of Estrella de Plata, delight in creating miniature dishes reflecting their interest in fusion food and contemporary trends. Elegant nibbles such as duck liver with hibiscus-flower syrup or tuna sashimi pizza are causing great excitement on the Barcelona food scene.

Spanish regional traditions have made their mark on Catalan eating habits.

BOQUERONES EN VINAGRE

CALAMARS A LA ROMANA

ESQUEIXADA DE BACALLÀ

PATATAS BRAVAS

BOQUERONES EN VINAGRE

The origins of this delicious tapa are uncertain, but it is now found all over Spain. Fresh anchovies are filleted, cured in vinegar and salt, and dressed with olive oil, finely chopped garlic, and parsley. The tangy vinegar marinade makes these little fish a perfect foil for a glass of cold Manzanilla or other fine dry sherry. Look for *boquerones* with firm white flesh, an indication of quality.

ESQUEIXADA DE BACALLÀ

Well-loved main courses featuring *bacallà,* salt cod, abound throughout Catalonia, and this popular salad is an adaptation of these classic dishes. Strips of salt cod (the verb *esqueixar* means "to shred") are tossed with roasted red sweet peppers, onions, tomatoes, and black olives. The resulting taste experience is a fine invention indeed: the saltiness of the cod is perfectly balanced by the sweetness of the sweet peppers. It is delicious paired with a glass of dry white wine.

CALAMARS A LA ROMANA

"Roman-style" squid rings are a timeless classic of Spanish bar-top snacking. But there is quite a difference in *calamars* dishes depending on where you go. Unscrupulous places cook up frozen pre-cooked squid, but honest establishments use only the fresh seafood, sliced, battered, and fried to sizzling crispness in olive oil. These light, crunchy, tender morsels are typically served with a sprinkling of salt and a wedge of lemon. For the perfect match, accompany them with a glass of beer or a jug of sangria.

PATATAS BRAVAS

Deep-fried potato chunks served with a spicy sauce, *patatas bravas* are a favourite snack food with students and young people, probably because they're both inexpensive and tasty. This satisfying dish is also a midday favourite with office and other workers who often wash it down with a glass of red wine. Originally hailing from Madrid, *patatas bravas* (the name means "brave potatoes") are now found in most Barcelona tapas bars.

CARGOLS

PERNIL IBÉRIC
(JAMÓN IBÉRICO)

CROQUETAS

BERBERECHOS

CARGOLS

To the Catalan gourmet, a bowlful of fresh snails is a thing of beauty. *Cargols* (*caracoles* in Spanish) are usually baked *a la llauna* (in a special tin) or cooked in a simple sauce with garlic, red sweet pepper, and perhaps a little blood sausage and a hint of chilli or cayenne pepper. To extract the snail from its shell, insert a tiny snail fork, the tip of a small knife, or a wooden toothpick as far inside the shell as you can and twist.

CROQUETAS

These golden brown croquettes originated as a tasty way to use up leftovers from the Sunday *carn d'olla* (meat stew), but they have become a classic snack food favoured all over Spain. They have a crispy crumb coating and are meltingly tender on the inside. *Croquetas* are most commonly made with ham or chicken or a combination, although inventive fillings based on ingredients such as wild mushrooms, prawns, and spinach are starting to appear at some of the more imaginative tapas bars in the city.

PERNIL IBÉRIC (JAMÓN IBÉRICO)

Cured ham from the Iberian pig is not made in Catalonia. It hails instead from the western regions of Andalusia and Extremadura, where the pigs roam the forests in a semi-wild state, feeding on acorns. But a product as good as this one was bound to be popular in Barcelona. *Pernil ibéric* is served in small slices cut directly from the ham at the moment of ordering. It makes a delicious tapa with beer or a glass of good red wine or *cava* (page 56).

BERBERECHOS

These are cockles, almost always canned in their own juices, and are a traditional accompaniment to the midday glass of vermouth. *Berberechos* are farmed in huge quantities in the estuaries off the western coast of Spain in Galicia, where they are fished by women known as *marisqueiras*. They are usually eaten by sprinkling with a squeeze of lemon, then spearing them with a toothpick.

The love of pork in all its forms is a touchstone for the people of the Iberian peninsula that dates back centuries, when its enthusiastic consumption was almost an article of faith. The *matanza*, or pig slaughter, is still celebrated once a year in rural homes, and the products resulting from it are as popular as ever.

XARCUTERIA

The love of meat, in particular ham and sausages, reaches near cult status in Spain. Nowhere is it better displayed than in Barcelona's popular *xarcuterias*, which are stocked with *pernils salats* (salt-cured hams) from the Pyrenees, *cansalada* (cured pork fat), a multitude of *embotits* (sausages), and other culinary treasures.

There are two basic types of sausage, cured and fresh. The latter consists principally of various kinds of *botifarra*: fat pork sausages meant to be grilled and served with beans, a dish known as *mongetes amb botifarra*; or parboiled sausages, including *botifarra blanca, botifarra negra* (blood sausage), and *botifarra catalana* (made with truffles and sweet wine). Of the cured sausages, the most famous is *salchichón*, also called *llonganissa*. The headquarters of

salchichón production is the town of Vic, which has a perfect climate for sausage curing – cold, dry, and misty – and a proud tradition stretching back at least two hundred years. The standard-bearer for *salchichón* quality in Vic is the house of Casa Sendra, founded in 1849 and still in operation. Casa Sendra employs a traditional process, using the best parts of the pig and curing them for five to nine months. The result is a meaty, firm-textured, and tasty slicing sausage.

Other Catalan pork specialities include *baldana de arròs* from the town of Tortosa, made with rice and a variety of nuts, and *pa de fetge,* a country pâté from the Cerdanya (page 83). The notoriously sweet *botifarra dolça* from the Empordà is made with sugar, lemon zest, cinnamon, and salt and is often served fried with apples.

Two destinations in Barcelona serve well for anyone wishing to sample these riches. The Botifarreria de Santa Maria is one of the city's prime pork butchers, stocking most of the Catalan specialities plus a fascinating range of original *botifarres,* featuring such ingredients as duck liver, fresh garlic, wild mushrooms, and the typically Catalan combination of spinach, pine nuts, and raisins. At La Cansaladeria, near the market in the urban village of Sants, master butcher Jordi Alsina presides as perhaps Barcelona's greatest expert on local pork cookery. He puts this knowledge into daily practice at his modestly sized shop, where he makes most of his *embotits* in the back. His *botifarra d'ou,* sausage with egg, is a delicious speciality worth seeking out if you happen to be in Barcelona at carnival time.

FUET

BOTIFARRA BLANCA

BOTIFARRA NEGRA

PERNIL SALAT
(JAMÓN SERRANO)

FUET

Long, thin, and dry-cured, this salami-like sausage is made with white wine, pepper, and spices. It often develops a natural white bloom on the surface. *Fuet* is a favourite for snacking, served, skinned and thinly sliced, with *pa amb tomàquet* (tomato-rubbed bread; page 75) or added to the packed lunches of schoolchildren. The sausages are almost certain to be found in the picnic basket of any Barcelonan heading out of town for the weekend.

BOTIFARRA BLANCA

This firm, white sausage has been produced for at least four hundred years. Mildly spiced, juicy, and aromatic, it is made with a mixture of lean meat and gelatinous cuts. Some Catalan *xarcuters* like to add egg to the mixture, in which case it becomes a *botifarra d'ou* – a speciality of carnival celebrations, especially in Barcelona. *Botifarra blanca* is usually seared, grilled, or fried and frequently accompanies *mongetes* (stewed white beans).

BOTIFARRA NEGRA

Botifarra negra is the Catalan version of blood sausage, those types made with fatty meat and blood. These blood puddings are known as *morcilla* elsewhere in Spain. They often contain chopped onion and spices such as cloves, black pepper, and allspice. Since they are parboiled, they can be thinly sliced and eaten without further cooking. More commonly, however, they are sliced, fried briefly, and served as part of a lunch dish, often with eggs and potatoes. *Botifarra negra* is also a vital ingredient in the classic dish *faves a la catalana* (page 113).

PERNIL SALAT (JAMÓN SERRANO)

This exceptional cured serrano ham, although not in the same league as the best Spanish *pernil ibéric* (page 37), is produced in the Pyrenean town of Olot. Though the qualities of a good serrano ham are not widely known outside Spain, they are increasingly appreciated. The rich, sweet-and-salty flavour makes it a natural partner for a dry sherry. Other excellent cured hams can be found outside Catalonia: Jabugo, Dehesa de Extremadura, and Guijuelo are Spain's three great areas of production for *ibéric* ham.

CATALANA

SALCHICHÓN DE VIC

BULL

SOBRASSADA

CATALANA

Many Catalan *embotits* have their equivalents in other parts of Spain. *Botifarra negra,* for example, resembles the blood sausage *morcilla de Burgos. Catalana,* however, is unique to Catalonia. According to some food historians, it may be the oldest of all Catalan sausages. Primarily made of lean meat, it has a firm texture and is generally large in size to make slicing easier. It is often flavoured with white wine or black pepper, or in luxurious versions, pieces of black truffle. *Catalana,* like *bull* (see right), makes a superb sandwich filling.

SALCHICHÓN DE VIC

Undoubtedly the best-known Catalan *embotit* – as well as the most prestigious and expensive – this speciality sausage, also called *llonganissa,* is one of the world's great pork products, equalled only by the finest locally made salami from Italy. It is best eaten in thin slices, typically with crusty bread or toast drizzled with olive oil. The recipe, as followed by artisanal producers in the town of Vic, is surprisingly simple; the only spices used are salt and pepper.

BULL

The name of this very classic Catalan sausage is derived from the Spanish verb *bullir,* which means "to boil". The raw materials consist mainly of pig offal, such as ears, trotters, and the meat of the pig's head and jaws. This gelatinous meat helps create the dense, sliceable texture of *bull.* The meat is coarsely chopped, mixed with spices and *pimentón,* and stuffed into sausage skins. The sausages are then boiled, cooled, and sliced thinly for eating in sandwiches, on toast, or as part of a mixed Catalan salad (page 122).

SOBRASSADA

Dry-curing meat is impossible in the hot, humid climate of the Mediterranean islands, so the people of Majorca, Ibiza, and Minorca developed a different technique: they add large amounts of *pimentón* (smoked paprika) to preserve the sausage meat for *sobrassada,* turning it bright orange in the process. *Sobrassada* is found in various forms – thick links in Majorca, thin links in Ibiza, or packed into small tubs. This delicious sausage is perfect with *pa amb tomàquet* (Tomato Rubbed Bread, page 75).

Olive oil is a cornerstone of all southern European cuisines, and *cuina catalana* is no exception. Celebrated for both its distinctive flavour and healthful properties, it is the basis for almost every savoury dish in the Catalan repertoire and is used generously throughout the Mediterranean diet.

OLIVE OIL

Olive oil is an essential ingredient in all the important sauces in Catalan cuisine, namely, *sofregit, romesco,* and *samfaina,* as well as the two eminent emulsion sauces, *maionesa* (mayonnaise) and *allioli* (garlic sauce). Drizzled over toasted bread that has been rubbed with tomato, it is an indispensable ingredient of *pa amb tomàquet* (page 75). It is even beginning to be used by some chefs in Barcelona as an element of the dessert course, in innovations such as chocolate-olive oil cookies and olive oil ice cream.

Olive oil is produced over a wide area of Catalonia, both on an industrial scale and in traditional *almazaras* (small estates). The most common cultivated olive variety is the Arbequina, famed for its exquisite delicacy of flavour. It is relatively small, roundish, and a delicate yellow-green when ripe. Other varieties grown in Catalonia include Farga, Morrut, Verdiell, Sevillenca, and Empeltre.

Catalonia is not the largest olive oil producer of the Spanish regions; that honour goes to Andalusia (where nearly 60 per cent of all the olive groves in the country are planted). But for quality, Catalonia's products are hard to surpass. Almost half of all Catalan olive oil is extra-virgin (derived without heat or chemicals from the first pressing) and is made predominantly from Arbequina olives.

Catalan olive oil also has far-reaching historical importance. In 1975, the oil-producing region of Les Garrigues, near Lleida, decided to create Europe's first-ever *Denominación de Origen* (DO) for olive oil. The new legislation enshrined in law the special qualities of Les Garrigues oil, such as its almondy, grassy fragrance. Two types are produced: *afruitat* (fruity), a thick, green oil from the early crop; and *dolç* (sweet), a yellow, more fluid oil. In 1977, the region of Siurana, near Tarragona, followed Les Garrigues in registering as a DO. Oils from Siurana's upland zone are tangy, smoky, and rich, while nearer the coast they are golden yellow and buttery smooth. Both areas continue to be pioneers in the production of single-estate, single-variety, and organic oils. Other important oil-producing DOs in Catalonia are Terra Alta and Baix Ebre.

Every estimable Barcelona grocer's sells a selection of Spanish olive oils, and local supermarkets such as Mercadona or Caprabo have a good Catalan selection. For the more expensive single-estate oils try the Corte Inglés shop on Plaça de Catalunya.

Making olive oil is only the final stage in a long process that begins with the planting of the trees. The best orchards in Catalonia are planted deep in well-drained soil. The young trees must be pruned, fertilised, irrigated, and treated for pests. In two or three years, they will begin to bear fruit, and the transformation of bitter, inedible olives into sweet, golden oil begins.

Olive Harvest

The olive harvest takes place in late autumn and winter, at which time the olive-growing areas of Catalonia become a frenzy of activity. Traditionally, trees were beaten with long poles so that the fruit fell into nets spread out on the ground. Nowadays, modern producers use mechanical shakers with long, vibrating arms in place of the sticks. Neither method is ideal, however, since the olive is a delicate fruit and prone to bruising. For a high-quality oil, the olives must be picked by hand.

Using Olive Oils

When using olive oil in the home kitchen, it's important to match the quality of the oil with the job at hand. In general, a good extra-virgin oil is best appreciated uncooked, in salad dressings and as a condiment for fish, freshly baked bread, or simple steamed vegetables. It is also drizzled on *pa amb tomàquet*, whereas a less intensely flavoured oil is used for frying. (Most Spanish cooks like to fry in abundant olive oil and reserve the oil for future use.) Note, however, the best *maionesa* (mayonnaise) does not call for extra-virgin oil, which can make the sauce too green and bitter. Virgin oil (see right) with perhaps a dash of stronger extra-virgin towards the end of the mixing process produces a mild, yet well-flavoured *maionesa*.

The issue of freshness is important in the case of olive oil, especially with the best oils that do not contain any preservatives. Olive oil is a surprisingly delicate product and can oxidise quickly once exposed to air and light. The best oils should be purchased as soon as possible after pressing and stored in a cool, dark place.

Making Olive Oil

PROCESSING AND GRINDING The olives are cleaned of dirt and leaves within a few hours of harvesting in order to preserve the polyphenols and flavour of the fruits. They are then ground, with stones left in, in a traditional stone mill or stainless-steel hammer mill.

PRESSING The resulting paste is spread out onto circular mats that are piled on top of one another and then pressed. Traditional presses used a single heavy tree trunk or a primitive hydraulic system made of cast iron. However, the state-of-the-art Sinolea separator, which extracts oil from the paste by means of stainless-steel blades, is gradually replacing Catalonia's traditional presses.

FLAVOURS AND CATEGORIES The first oil to run from the presses is defined as extra virgin. Subsequent untreated pressings are called virgin oil. Finally, the paste is treated chemically to extract the remaining oil, and this yield is often blended with oil from other batches to create *aceite de oliva puro,* an oil that is lighter in flavour and color and more fluid than the initial pressings.

It would be hard to overestimate the importance of seafood in Catalan cuisine. You could remove the meat dishes and it would still be a worthwhile and varied cuisine; remove the fish dishes, however, and you take away its heart and soul.

SEAFOOD

Fish in Catalonia was traditionally associated with fasting and particularly with Lent, a time of year when meat was banned from the menu. Some fish types, particularly salt cod, still maintain this link with religion. But as Spain's commitment to Catholicism has waned, so has its attitude toward penitence. Nowadays, virtually everyone knows the health benefits of fresh fish, and Catalan fish markets are busier than ever.

La cuina catalana uses fish in a broad range of cooking techniques, from frying and boiling to roasting and barbecuing *a la brasa* (over coals). Some of Catalonia's most delicious preparations of white fish, such as grouper and gilthead bream, involve baking the whole fish in the oven, either encased in rock salt (page 161) or laid on a bed of thinly sliced vegetables such as potatoes and red sweet peppers, generously sluiced with olive

oil. Seafood mixed with rice is an equally classic combination along the entire Mediterranean coast, and it sometimes takes unusual forms. *Arròs negre* uses squid ink to turn the dish a sumptuous shade of purplish black, whereas *rossejat* calls for browning the rice in the pan before adding the fish and stock.

It seems that all Mediterranean cuisines have at least one mixed fish soup or stew to their name. Catalan cooking has several. Best known of all is the *suquet,* a simple combination of potatoes and rockfish with a *picada* of almonds and garlic, closely followed by the *sarsuela,* a popular dish in Barcelona that includes a variety of shellfish. Then there are the *romesco* of Tarragona with its almond-hazelnut sauce, the *simitomba* of the Costa Brava (monkfish and potatoes with a thick topping of *allioli*), and the *all cremat* of

Vilanova, featuring lots of toasted garlic. *Bacallà* (salt cod) is an oddity among the fish species found in Barcelona's markets, since cod is generally caught in the cold waters of Iceland or the Faroe Islands and salted for export to Spain and Portugal. Catalan cooking has at least a dozen popular recipes for *bacallà,* including Barcelona's famous *bacallà a la llauna* (oven roasted in a special tin), *bunyols de bacallà* (fritters), and, most classically, with *samfaina* sauce (page 141).

An oddity of a different kind is the Catalan tendency to mix seafood and meat in the same dish, resulting in heady delights known as *mar i muntanya* (page 149).

You can find these riches at the many *peixateries* (fishmongers) in the city. The most plentiful seafood destination is the fish section of La Boqueria (page 25), and the venerable Ricart, a fish shop located in the Barceloneta

Catalan fishmongers take great pride in the rich variety of their wares.

ORADA / DORÁDA
5'70
€/Kg

A FEIRA

0'60 €uros

CALAMARS

ESCAMARLANS

GAMBES

MUSCLOS

ESCAMARLANS

Escamarlans (*langostinos* in Spanish, langoustines or Dublin Bay prawns) are frequently confused with their undersea cousins, *gambes* (prawns). They are paler in colour and have a more delicate flavour and firmer, meatier texture. The Spanish regard *escamarlans* as superior to prawns and are prepared to pay a much higher price for them at the market – especially during the festivals, when they are traditionally prepared. They are often served cold, with *allioli* on the side.

GAMBES

Juicy and bursting with the flavour of the sea, *gambes,* prawns, are a favourite food of Barcelonans. They are cooked *a la planxa* (on a griddle, page 95) or *a la brasa* (over coals), or briefly fried in olive oil. Eat them Spanish style: first snap off their heads and suck out the juices, then peel off the shell from the rest of the body. For the best of the best, seek out the prawns of Palamós and Roses, two small coastal towns north of Barcelona; these *gambes* are famous for their creamy and succulent character.

CALAMARS

Calamars a la romana, battered, deep-fried squid rings, is the classic Spanish treatment for this popular seafood. Squid are also commonly cooked *a la planxa,* simmered with potatoes and onions, or, in the Empordá, stuffed with ham, egg, and an almond *picada.* In elegant restaurants, the menu often features the term *de pote,* meaning that the squid has been caught by the traditional hook-and-line method as opposed to the invasive commercial techniques that bruise and damage the delicate flesh.

MUSCLOS

Spanish *musclos,* or mussels, come mainly from the cool waters of Galicia, where they are farmed in the estuaries of the Rias Baixas. Once in Catalonia, they typically find their way into some type of rice dish, or sometimes they are prepared *a la planxa* and tossed with parsley and garlic. A popular tapa in Barcelona presents the cold, cooked mussel in its shell, dressed with a vinegary *pipirrana* of diced red and green sweet peppers and tomato.

ORADA

ESCÓRPORA

SARDINES

ANXOVA

ORADA

The *orada* (*dorada* in Spanish) is distinguished from similar species of fish by a small golden patch just above the eyes; hence, the English name, gilthead bream (*orada* and *dorada* both mean "golden"). Once an expensive and much sought-after fish, it is now more affordable, thanks to the rise of *piscifactorias* (fish farms) along the Mediterranean coast. The *orada* is the classic choice for baking whole in the oven, most commonly *a la sal* (in a salt crust; page 161) or on a bed of potatoes and onions.

ESCÓRPORA

The *escórpora,* or scorpion fish, is a common sight in the fish markets of Barcelona and in other Mediterranean cities (such as Marseilles, where it is used in bouillabaisse). *Scorpaena scrofa* is an unprepossessing creature, red and covered with fierce-looking spines that are poisonous to the touch – even when the fish is dead. A rockfish that lives close to the shoreline, the *escórpora* is highly valued by Catalan cooks for its rich flavour and gelatinous flesh. It is considered a vital ingredient in any good fish stock.

SARDINES

Few smells are more evocative than that of fresh sardines barbecuing over an open fire. These small, silvery fish are at their best from June to September, when they are especially fat and meaty. The fish are celebrated in a food fiesta known as *sardinada popular* and held in Calella on the coast near Girona. This is a grand celebration (usually in mid-May) of barbecued sardines served with *pa amb tomàquet* (tomato-rubbed bread, page 75) and washed down with plenty of local wine.

ANXOVA

Anchovies marinated in olive oil, parsley, and vinegar, or *boquerones en vinagre*, are regularly seen in Barcelona bars. They are also served deep-fried, either whole or in fillets. But most commonly they are salted and canned in olive oil, then eaten as a snack on toast, in salads such as *xató* (page 109), or as a topping for savoury *coques* (flatbreads). The most prestigious salted anchovy preparations in Spain, those of L'Escala near Girona, raise this humble fish to the level of a true delicacy.

As is typical in southern European society, wine is an important part of life in Catalonia. No meal is complete without a glass or two, and even children are sometimes given a drop of wine to taste. It is seen as a natural part of a civilised lifestyle.

CATALAN WINE

The grapevine is, with the olive tree, the most characteristic element of Spain's landscape. It grows throughout the length and breadth of the country and produces wines of every imaginable type. Spain has more land devoted to vineyards than any other country in the world, with a staggering 1.2 million hectares (2.9 million acres), although it is considered only the third most important wine producer, after France and Italy.

The vineyards of Catalonia represent a variety in terms of vine types and ages. Fifty years ago, most of the vineyards in this region were planted with traditional Spanish grape varieties, such as Macabeu, Ull de Lebre, Garnatxa, and Parellada. But in recent years, growers have been influenced by New World grapes and now Merlot, Chardonnay, and Cabernet have been introduced.

Even though historically Catalonia has not been known as a major wine-growing area, Catalan wines were some of the first made on the Iberian peninsula, pressed from the fruit of vines planted by the ancient Greeks in their colony at Empúries. In the 1950s, most Catalan wine was poor stuff indeed, considered peculiar and somewhat primitive. Even until the 1970s, most of the local wine was sold in bulk. People would take their bottles to the wineshop, or *bodega,* and fill them straight from the barrel. Wine was either drunk at home, as an accompaniment to the large midday meal, or swigged from thick glasses in small, gloomy bars into which women never ventured.

In those days, even though vast amounts of wine were produced, most of it was of dubious quality. The plains of the Spanish provinces of Castille La Mancha and Murcia, near the town of Jumilla, were the source of industrial quantities of basic table wine – certainly not the kind of wine most Spaniards would drink today. Without the benefit of temperature control, fermentation took place at a tremendous speed, effectively burning off the delicate fruit aromas and subtle nuances of the grapes. Spanish reds and whites alike were all too often thinly flavoured, lacking body, oxidised and too alcoholic – the classic "hot country" wine of the past, now consigned to history.

Change started in the 1960s, with the success of Torres, the principal wine family of the Penedès – an esteemed wine-growing region south of Barcelona – whose table wines were modern products with a world-wide appeal. Since then, Catalan wine has

Catalan wine has a history stretching back to the ancient Greeks.

never ceased improving, and some of the sleepiest areas in the past – the prime example being Priorat – now produce some of the finest wines in the world.

Catalonia now produces every type of wine, from reds, whites, and rosés to sparkling wines (known as *cavas*), fortified wines, muscats, and local specialities such as *vi d'agulla* ("needle wine", so named for its slightly prickly taste), and the oxidised *vi ranci*.

The region possesses eleven of the sixty-two Spanish *Denominacions de Origen* (DO) for wine. The DO is a system of controls that states that certain wines may be made only in demarcated areas, from particular grape

also be made of *cava* – Spain's highly regarded sparkling wine, made in the town of Sant Sadurní d'Anoia.

Given the importance of wine in Catalan culture, it has taken a surprisingly long time for œnology, as a subject deserving of expertise, as well as enjoyment, to take root in Barcelona. But the city is quickly making up for lost time. La Vinya del Senyor, in the shadow of the basilica of Santa Maria del Mar, was one of the first wine bars in Barcelona and remains one of the best. Its extensive wine list, with more than three hundred options, is updated regularly. When in Barcelona, check out La Vinya del Senyor's new branch in the Sarrià district, which has fine tapas as

Catalonia is a pioneer in the use of old vines to make wines of great concentration and power – a prime example is the Priorat region, where some vines are over sixty years old.

varieties and using specific techniques. The eleven Catalan DOs range from the huge and commercially muscular Penedès, probably the most dynamic of all Catalonia's wine regions, to the small yet outstanding Alella, a tiny area of just over five hundred hectares (1200 acres). The DOs in between are of all types, from the exclusive Priorat, whose revolutionary wines have taken the international wine world by storm, to relatively humble and little-known names like Conca de Barberà and Pla de Bages. Tarragona, a region south-east of Priorat, has been planted in vineyards since the days of the Roman Empire, when the local products were shipped to Rome's well-to-do residents. The Greeks were the first to recognise the rich soil of Empordà–Costa Brava, today a source of well-regarded dessert wines and rosés. Looking to the future of Spanish wine, up-and-coming DOs include the regions of Montsant and Terra Alta. Mention should

well as a standard à la carte menu. With an extensive wine list from around the world, Cata 1.81 is one of the most fashionable of the new breed of wine bar, with a striking design and an interesting menu of *raciones,* light meals, to accompany them. Barcelona's *xampanyeries* (sparkling wine bars) are an excellent way to sample a variety of local *cavas.* El Xampanyet is perhaps the best known and popular, having been in operation since the 1930s.

The increasing local interest in regional and international wines is also reflected in some exceptional wine merchants, notably Viniteca, an old-town boutique owned by the genial Quim Vila, whose knowledge of Spanish wine is practically encyclopedic; and Lavinia, possibly Barcelona's largest wine emporium and almost certainly its most complete, especially where Catalan wines are concerned. All eleven DOs are represented, and the range, as well as the design and atmosphere of the shop, is quite impressive.

The process of making wine in Catalonia is essentially the same as it is in the rest of Spain and Europe. It follows the rhythm of the year, beginning in the depths of winter when the vines are pruned and cared for, continuing through the summer when the grapes ripen, and culminating in autumn when, in a burst of activity, the harvest takes place and the grapes are crushed.

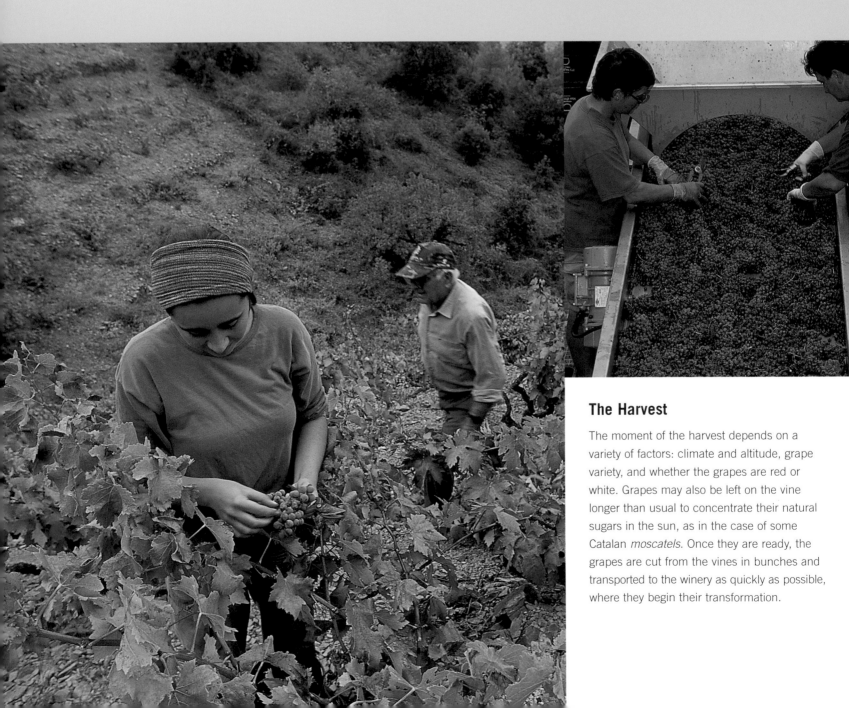

The Harvest

The moment of the harvest depends on a variety of factors: climate and altitude, grape variety, and whether the grapes are red or white. Grapes may also be left on the vine longer than usual to concentrate their natural sugars in the sun, as in the case of some Catalan *moscatels*. Once they are ready, the grapes are cut from the vines in bunches and transported to the winery as quickly as possible, where they begin their transformation.

Catalan Wine Dynasties

The story of Catalan wine is one of history, tradition, and economic influence. Nobody knows this better than the dynasties that have dominated *el vi català* over time – in some cases for hundreds of years. The greatest names in Catalan wine are those of families that have built up powerful businesses around their own vineyards and cellars. The Torres family of the Penedès is known throughout the world as the creators of a great wine empire. Another pre-eminent name is Raventós, the influential family behind the Codorníu label, whose *cava* is one of the most popular in Spain. The family bottled its first sparkling wines in the 1870s, many of which they despatched to the royal family in Madrid. The Ferrer family of Freixenet, another highly regarded sparkling wine producer, also boasts a company history that goes back to the nineteenth century. Finally, the Gramona family represents a Penedès wine dynasty that has recently shot to fame as a producer of modern wines such as Gessami, Chardonnay, Más Escorpí, and the ice wine Vi de Gel.

Making Wine

CRUSH AND EXTRACTING Once harvested, the grapes are destemmed and crushed, then juice is extracted in a press, although red grapes are sometimes left whole to ferment. The traditional method of pressing with the feet is now quite rare, although it is occasionally seen in rural settings.

FERMENTING Next, the juice undergoes fermentation, the process by which the sugars in the grape juice are converted into alcohol by the yeasts occurring naturally on the grape skins. This is usually done in large stainless-steel vats and takes around fifteen days, after which the wine is cloudy and is left to settle until it is clear.

RACKING AND BOTTLING After fermentation, wine is then usually "racked", poured off from the tanks and separated from the sediment that settles at the bottom. This allows the wine to breathe. Racking may occur several times before the wine is ready to bottle. It is then filtered, bottled, and ready for ageing or selling.

CAVA

ALELLA

CHARDONNAY

PENEDÈS WHITE

CAVA

Spain's cheerful national fizz has never claimed to have the slightest rivalry with French champagne – despite the fact that *cava* is known in Spain as *champán*. The truth is that the two are very different wines, champagne being acknowledged as the superior product. Still, the quality of *cava* has soared in recent years, and the best dry vintages are delicious. This sparkler is often associated with celebrations, such as weddings and birthdays, and is also served during the festive Christmas season with *turróns* (almond nougat).

ALELLA

This wine, essentially Barcelona's "house white", has been popular with the Catalan nobility since the Middle Ages. The typical Alella is a mild, easy-to-drink wine, refreshingly light and fruity, the perfect choice to accompany seafood.

CHARDONNAY

While local varieties like Parellada, Macabeo, Verdejo, and Airen are still the most popular whites, New World grape varieties such as Chardonnay and Sauvignon Blanc are gaining ground following the increasing influence of wines from California and Australia.

PENEDÈS WHITE

Thanks to skillful marketing, the white wine of the Penedès represents what a Spanish white wine should be: lively and full-bodied, yet well-balanced and packed with fruit. The archetypal Penedès white is arguably Gran Viña Sol from Torres, made with the Parellada grape variety and firmed up with a dose of Chardonnay. Other Penedès whites blended with the Chardonnay grape have also shot to international fame – especially Milmanda from Torres, widely regarded as one of Spain's finest white wines.

RIOJA

Rioja is Spain's best-known wine, both within the country and abroad. Despite Catalonia's loyalty to its own vintages, a good Rioja commands a great deal of respect in Barcelona. A glass of this oaky, velvety red wine, made from the Tempranillo and Garnacha grape varieties, is the perfect pairing with a plate of ham, cheese, and sausages. The word *reserva* on a bottle of Rioja means it has aged for at least three years, with one year in oak barrels; *gran reserva* means five years of ageing, two of those years in oak.

PRIORAT RED

PENEDÈS RED

RIOJA

VI RANCI

MOSCATEL

PENEDÈS RED

The most popular red wines in Barcelona hail from the Penedès region, producer both of fruity and unassuming reds and superb, exquisitely made reds such as Mas La Plana from Torres, an all-Cabernet wine that famously beat out Château Latour in a 1979 tasting. Red grape varieties grown in the Penedès include Ull de Llebre and Garnacha, although "foreign" varieties like Cabernet Sauvignon and Merlot are now successfully being used in conjunction.

PRIORAT RED

Dark, thick, and strong – that was the way Priorat was always thought of in the past, so much so that the wines were barely drunk in Spain but were instead sent in bulk to France for blending. Once a little-known inland district, ravaged by poverty and depopulation, the Priorat has undergone a radical transformation thanks to a handful of dedicated young winemakers. The potent wines of Priorat are now recognised internationally. Because they are expensive, however, they are generally brought out only on special occasions.

VI RANCI

This slightly oxidised, mildly sweet red wine is a traditional product aged in barrels at a higher temperature than normal to allow for natural oxidation to take place. It was commonly drunk as an *aperitiu* (aperitif) or digestif (in the small villages of Catalonia it doubtless still is) but is now mainly used in cooking. It is a common addition to meat stews, roasts, and pasta sauces. Well-known makers of *vi ranci* are deMuller in Tarragona and Scala Dei in the Priorat.

MOSCATEL

Catalans have a sweet tooth and like nothing better than a glass of sweet wine at the end of a meal with dessert, in the afternoon with pastries and cakes, or even as an aperitif. *Moscatel,* a sweet, raisiny wine, is sometimes served in a *porrón,* a long-spouted glass drinking vessel, and often accompanies the platter of nuts and dried fruit known as *postre del músic* (page 173). Some of the best *moscatels* come from Alicante, in the far south of the Catalan lands.

In the 1990s, a new generation of Catalan artisans set out to learn the ancient techniques of Spanish cheese-making, with promising results. Many of these pioneers are self-taught and most are based in small, remote villages deep in the countryside.

FORMATGE

Catalonia is prime dairy country. The Mediterranean zone has richly varied flora of aromatic herbs and flowers, perfect for goats, and the foothills of the Pyrenees are permanently lush with grass, making them an ideal habitat for cows. In fact, the traditionally made cheese of Alt Urgell-Cerdanya, a superb cow's milk cheese from the Pyrenees, was recently awarded *Denominación de Origen* status, making it the first Catalan cheese to gain this much-coveted recognition.

Three important figures in the artisan cheese movement in Catalonia are Jordi Conejero, whose Suau de Clúa is one of the best new Catalan cheeses (look for his stall at the Plaça del Pi market in Barcelona on the first Saturday and Sunday of every month); Francesc Buscallà, maker of Baridà,

a fine goat's milk cheese; and Eulàlia Torres in Ossera, near Tarragona, creator of Serrat Gros, one of the best goat's milk cheeses in Spain. Montsec, another notable "alternative" cheese, was invented in 1978 by a group of young people in the formerly abandoned village of Clúa, in the province of Lleida.

There are a number of good cheese shops in Barcelona, and more and more artisanal products are being stocked every year. Scottish-born Katherine McLaughlin has a small but exquisite selection of Spanish farmhouse cheeses at her little shop, called Formatgeria la Seu, in the Barri Gòtic, and is always on the lookout for local fresh cheeses. She regularly carries the superb washed-rind Tou de Tillers "Roi", as well as Aitona, Suau de Clúa, and Tabollet. Not far away, in the

Born district, is Tot Formatges, which stocks cheeses from France, Italy, and Germany as well as Spain. Another purveyor of local cheeses is Tutusaus, an upmarket deli in the Sarrià area, where you can sit in a dining area to enjoy the shop's fine smoked salmon, *embotits* (sausages), and other delicacies as well as wonderful cheeses.

For perhaps the best cheese shop in Catalonia, however, you will have to head outside the city to the Pyrenees. Eugene Celery, owner of Formatgeria Eugene in La Seu d'Urgell, is a master *affineur* (cheese ager and seller) worthy of the best in France. In addition to a fine range of cheeses from across the French border, he stocks most of the new-wave Spanish Pyrenean cheeses, including Baridà, Serrat Gros, and Nevat.

Thanks to young, innovative craftspeople, the future looks bright for Catalan cheese.

MAHÓN SEMI-SEC

MAHÓN SEC

MATÓ DE
MONTSERRAT

TOU DELS TILLERS

MAHÓN SEMI-SEC

Small brown cows grazing between rambling stone walls are a distinctive feature of the landscape of Minorca. The dairy cow was brought to Catalonia by the British in the eighteenth century, so it is not surprising that the island's signature cheese, Mahón, resembles England's famous cow's milk Cheddar. The distinctive square shape comes from the practise of tying the curds in large square cloths to drain. Mahón semi-sec, aged for six months or less, is a young, firm-textured, mild cheese with a pronounced yellow colour.

MAHÓN SEC

Mahón is a single type of cheese that changes in flavour and texture depending on the length of time it matures. Aged in cool cellars for up to a year, Mahón sec becomes dry *(sec)* and hard and loses some of its buttercup yellow colour. The flavour transformation during ageing is striking. Starting out mild and creamy, the cheese becomes intensely flavoured, salty, and nutty, with a piquant edge. Mahón sec is often grated over vegetables or pasta or used on a cheese platter, paired with Madeira or tawny Port.

TOU DELS TILLERS

The maker of Tou dels Tillers, Enric Canut, is a well-respected expert on Spanish cheeses. Tou dels Tillers is a Brie-like product with a chalky white skin, runny interior, and mildly creamy flavour. It is made from raw cow's milk near the mountain town of Sort in the province of Lleida. This lightly salty cheese is excellent accompanied by a young red wine such as those from the Empordà or perhaps a rosé from Cigales. It is also often used in cooking.

MATÓ DE MONTSERRAT

Mató is the Catalan name for a simple, fresh cheese no more than a few days old. It is often made from cow's milk, but sheep's milk versions are also readily available. Hugely popular all over the region, it is eaten with honey as a dessert or for breakfast, or it is used in cooking, for example, in sweet cheese tarts such as *flaó* (page 177). The best-known *mató* is made in Montserrat, near Barcelona.

CABRA AMB PEBRE

GARROTXA

FORMATGE DE CABRA EN OLI D'OLIVA

SUAU DE CLÚA

FORMATGE DE CABRA EN OLI D'OLIVA

In order to mature, cheese needs air, so if you take away the oxygen, the process is dramatically slowed down. Catalans have a particular preference for fresh, young cheeses over aged, strongly-flavoured ones, which sometimes leads them to ingenious solutions. When a cheese is just a few days old, and firm enough to handle but not completely solid, it can be rolled into logs, sliced into "buttons", and immersed in extra-virgin olive oil. This way, the fresh cheese keeps for weeks, while taking on the fruity richness of the olive oil.

CABRA AMB PEBRE

During the process of drying and curing, cheese naturally forms a rind. Over the centuries, Europe's cheese-makers discovered that rubbing the cheese with certain products, such as chilli pepper, wood ash, or ground black pepper, not only helped the rind to form but also preserved the cheese from attack by bacteria that might alter the taste or infect the cheese with harmful toxins. Pepper is rubbed over goat cheese for *cabra amb pebre,* a popular preparation in Catalonia. The peppery oils preserve the cheese and impart a spiciness to its mild creaminess.

SUAU DE CLÚA

High in the Montsec mountains is the tiny village of Clúa – population thirty-two – where a few young craftspeople have settled to live and work. The man behind Clúa cheese is Jordi Conejero, who first created it twenty years ago. Suau de Clúa cheese comes in flatish rounds. Made from raw goat's milk, it is sometimes presented with a coating of ash and is matured for sixty to ninety days. In its two decades of life, Clúa cheese has gained in popularity and prestige, becoming one of the most famous of the new generation of Catalan cheeses.

GARROTXA

This goat's cheese is commonly known in Catalonia as *formatge pell florida* (literally, "flowery skin cheese") because of the grey bloom that forms spontaneously on the rind. It was originally made in flat, circular clay moulds and is still faithfully produced in that shape. The two-pound (1-kg) cheeses are allowed to mature briefly, for about two weeks, to develop a softly unctuous, buttery texture. A layer of wood ash is sometimes added to the rind to help to stabilise and preserve the cheese. Garrotxa is notable for its faint hazelnut aftertaste.

In the towns and cities of Catalonia, the *pastisseria* is an institution. Every moment of the day provides an opportunity to visit – from morning croissants and midday slices of *coca* to afternoon *berenars* and elaborate desserts fit for any celebration.

PASTISSERIES

There is more to the *pastisseries* – patisseries or cake shops – of Catalonia than their name implies. Of course, cakes, pastries, and biscuits are their main stock in trade, but many of them also have specialities that set them apart from their competition. Some *pastisseries* have branched out into sweet or savoury *coques* (flatbreads), which are usually the territory of the *forns* (bread ovens). Others are known for their croissants, chocolate bonbons, *crema catalana* (burnt custard, page 170), or their expertise with sweets from elsewhere, such as panettone or plum cake. Some are more like sweet shops, others mainly bakeries. The *pastisseria* is in essence simply a dispensary of good things to eat that are mainstays of the Catalan table but that require too much time or skill (or both) for most people to make at home.

Given the decline of interest in church-going in contemporary Spain, it's surprising how much influence Roman Catholicism still has over daily lives. For example, nearly every Catalan pastry and biscuit has its place in the religious calendar, from the *tortell de Reis* made for the feast of Epiphany and the *coca de Sant Joan* for the Feast of St John to the *turróns* and *neules* for Christmas. This calendar is strictly adhered to; it's useless to look for *mona de Pasqua* (chocolate Easter cake, page 174) in November, for example, or *panellets* (nut biscuits, page 80) in April.

By and large, Catalan baking, like the food in general, is not characterised by subtlety or great refinement. Its strength resides in the skill with which even the simplest pastry can be made to taste delicious. The basis of the repertoire is a rich brioche dough, and the difference between one speciality and the next is mainly in the variety of fillings and toppings. It has been further elevated by the influence of nearby France, and almost all *pastissers* now use butter, instead of the more traditional lard, in their cakes. (Vegetarians take note: *llardons*, pork cracklings, are usually added to the dough for the *coca de Sant Joan* and *coca de Sant Jaume*.)

When in Barcelona, it is worth visiting some of the city's *pastisseries*. Five of the best are Escribà, Foix, Brunells, Baixas, and Sacha. They are not only sumptuously decorated but also enormously popular, and it's not uncommon to see queues snaking out into the street. If your purchase is a gift, say so (*"es per regalar"*) and it will be packed in a beribboned box at no extra charge.

BORREGUETS
SANT ANTONI
2'00€ bolsa

PANELLETS
assortits

Sweet and savoury treats draw crowds at Barcelona's finest *pastisseries*.

BRUNEL

The *coca* is Catalonia's most famous pastry. It takes many forms, both sweet and savoury, from the roast vegetable-topped *coca de recapte* (page 76) to the sugary *coca de vidre* (page 91). *Les coques* are popular foods all year long but are particularly abundant during the many religious processions and the parties held during Carnival.

Types of Coques

The word *coca* signals a pastry base. From the popular *coca de recapte,* topped with anything from sweet peppers to salted herrings to sausages, to the typical Balearic Islands' *coca,* topped with spinach, pine nuts, and raisins, what characterises *coques* is variety. They can be sweet or savoury, topped with cinnamon and lemon, crystallised fruit, nuts, cheese, mushrooms, ham, anchovies, tuna, and tomatoes. Others are filled with such delectables as grated pumpkin or custard.

Escribà

Tourists walking down the Ramblas market street in the heart of Barcelona often stop in amazement at the jewel-like Pastisseria Escribà. The beautiful gold-and-green art nouveau shopfront acts as a magnet for anyone interested in early-twentieth-century design. Once you enter the shop, however, academic concerns take second place to appetite. Escribà is a treasure trove of fine sweets, both local and foreign, with a bounty of almond biscuits, sugary *coques* studded with pine nuts, and specialities like *brazo de gitano* (gypsy's arm), a cream-and-sponge-cake roulade, or *rambla,* a sponge-and-chocolate truffle cake. The members of the Escribà family are the aristocrats of Barcelona *pastissers.* The firm was founded in 1906, and Antoni Escribà, the founder, is as famous in Catalonia as chef Ferran Adrià of El Bulli. He even has his own entry in the Catalan national encyclopedia, which describes him as "A man of great culture and sensibility".

Making Coca de Llardons

MAKING THE PASTRY *Coca de llardons* is the quintessential Catalan *coca,* simple and delicious when freshly made with the best materials. The basic ingredients are flour, butter or lard, minced pork fat or *panceta* (the *llardons*), sugar, and pine nuts. First, the dough – flour, butter or lard, salt, and water – is mixed, then kneaded by hand.

ROLLING AND DIVIDING Next, the dough is rolled out into a thin sheet, the *llardons* are sprinkled on top, and the dough is folded over and rolled out again. It is then divided into pieces, and each

piece is then rolled out one last time into an elongated strip with rounded ends – the shape of the classic Catalan *coca.*

FINISHING AND BAKING The shaped pastries are finally brushed with melted lard or butter and generously sprinkled with sugar and pine nuts. They are then baked at a high temperature until the sugary topping is browned and crispy, which takes about 20 minutes. The *coca de llardons* is best eaten warm, with a steaming cup of hot chocolate or coffee, or a glass of sparkling *cava. Salut!*

The love affair between Barcelona and chocolate has been going on for centuries. The city has had a close and fulfilling relationship with *xocolata* since at least 1759, when Carlos III arrived from Naples in a galleon and handed out gifts of chocolate powder to the crew members as a sign of gratitude.

XOCOLATA

The custom of enjoying chocolate as a beverage is a deep-rooted one that is still very much alive in Catalonia. Drinking chocolate is thick and sweet, just right for dunking *churros* (long fried pastries), *magdalenas* (madeleines), or, most typically in Barcelona, *melindros,* sponge cakes topped with icing.

Chocolate in Catalonia has some more unpredictable uses. For example, it may appear in a stuffing for squid, and it forms part of the *picada* used in the complex *mar i muntanya* dishes of northern Catalonia (see page 149). Unsweetened chocolate is grated into game stews as well, to which it adds a rich smokiness and helps thicken the liquid.

Chocolate bars are very popular in Catalonia, though perhaps not eaten in the quantities they are in northern Europe. Brunells, a *pastisseria* founded in 1852 and

whose original wood-fired oven is still in use, sells a brown paper-wrapped chocolate bar containing 75 per cent cocoa mass made from beans from Venezuela, Ecuador, and Grenada. Other well-known local brands are Solé, Simon Coll, Blanxart, Xoco-Ter, Ludomar, and Cudié. The last is also famous for its bonbons.

A quiet revolution in sweet-eating is taking place in and around Barcelona. The city is discovering, along with the joys of eating and drinking fine chocolate, the praline, the truffle, and the handmade chocolate bar. A culture is developing, one that puts increasing emphasis on quality and craft. Shops such as Xocoa and Cacao Sampaka (the latter calls itself *El Nou Mercat del Cacao*) offer chocolate lovers an exciting and appetising mixture of design and gastronomic

thrills, including truffles flavoured with balsamic vinegar, olive oil, hazelnuts, and even anchovies! Elda, a town in southern Valencia, boasts one of Europe's finest chocolatiers, Paco Torreblanca, winner of many awards for his exquisite workmanship. Chocovic, a shop making *couverture* and fine eating chocolate in the town of Vic, is shaping up as a worthy competitor to French firms such as Valrhona.

Chic chocolate desserts are all the rage in Barcelona. There are few cities in the world where a restaurant serving only desserts (the most famous being Espai Sucre, run by chef Jordi Butrón) could be such a smash hit. Also at the height of fashion, Oriol Balaguer's new "showroom" as he calls his workshop in Barcelona, is a minimalist temple to the exquisite art of chocolate-making.

Chocolate culture in Barcelona is a combination of the traditional and the avant-garde.

Chocolate truffles and other soft-centred sweets have always been popular in Barcelona, and a box of beautiful chocolates is frequently brought as a gift when dining at a friend's home. The city's new-wave chocolate shops, such as Xocoa, havc taken the traditional Barcelonan *bonbon*, reduced it in size, and transformed it into an elegant, exquisitely made, expensive delicacy.

Changing chocolate culture

The culture of chocolate in Barcelona has grown dramatically in the last ten years. In the old days, chocolate came in two basic forms—*chocolate a la taza,* a slab of bitter chocolate to be grated and mixed with water or milk for drinking, and the traditional truffle. Modern tastes have changed. Barcelona now prefers its chocolate in the form of a bar, strongly flavoured and bitter – 75 per cent, 85 per cent, and even 100 per cent cocoa mass are possible.

Xocoa

Although it might not look like it from the ultramodern design of each of the shops, Xocoa is one of Barcelona's oldest chocolate firms with a history going back to 1897, when the Escursell family established its first shop in the Barceloneta neighborhood.

Nowadays, the business is run by grandsons Miquel and Marc, who have three shops located around the city and a restaurant specialising in both sweet and savoury crepes. The restaurant is notable for both the food and its design, particularly the elegant "white chocolate" chairs. The brothers have branched out daringly from the traditional repertoire of truffles and pastries into novelties like herb- and spice-flavoured chocolates, chocolate-and-saffron mousse, and chilli-spiced chocolates, and they also sell candles and incense infused with cocoa. Their chocolate CDs (sold in proper CD jewel boxes) have been a notable hit with clients. Marc and Miquel now plan to make *monas de Pasqua* (chocolate Easter cakes, page 174) with famed local chocolate designer Jordi Labanda.

Making Chocolate Bonbons

MIXING THE FILLING For a classic chocolate bonbon, the first task is to mix the filling, usually either an almond-based praline or a rich ganache of cream and cocoa powder with added flavourings. The mixture is spread out on trays to cool, then cut to the required size.

TEMPERING The next step is to make the chocolate coating for the bonbon. *Couverture* ("covering" in French), a baking chocolate high in cocoa butter, is used. It must be tempered by heating it to 40°–45°C (104°–113°F) then cooled by spreading the melted chocolate on a marble slab. Tempering gives the chocolate an attractive shine and consistent colour.

DIPPING AND FINISHING The *couverture* is now melted again so that the bite-sized squares of filling can be hand-dipped in the chocolate. Some bonbons are left plain; others are sprinkled with cocoa powder, nuts, gold leaf, or other decorations. Finally, the bonbons are left to cool and set.

BERENARS I TAPAS

From sweet to savoury, snacks and hors d'oeuvres such as marinated sardines, empanadas, and pine nut biscuits offer convenience in a fast-paced city.

Food in Barcelona is often a movable feast, to be eaten on the go. One prime source of "fast food" is the *pastisseria,* or patisserie (page 62), for the sweet foods Catalans crave at all hours of the day and for savoury *berenars* (snacks) such as *coca de recapte,* flatbread with any number of toppings. The tapas bar, although not traditional in Catalonia, is now a fixture among Barcelonans who appreciate the convenience of this unique style of Spanish eating. *Berenars* may even challenge the supremacy of a regular three-course meal. A simple, delicious repast can be made from *pa amb tomàquet,* a slice of ham, and slabs of cheese and quince paste.

PA AMB TOMÀQUET

Tomato-rubbed Bread

Bread and tomato – how something so simple and apparently artless could have come to such importance is one of the mysteries of Catalan food. More than just a dish, pa amb tomàquet is a badge of Catalonian identity. Although it can be served year-round, it is particularly good in summer, when tomatoes are ripe, sweet, and bright red, and in winter, when fresh olive oil is running off the presses and still has its fruity taste and golden colour. Pa amb tomàquet makes a brilliant party food when served with salami, pâté, and cheese.

1 Prepare a fire in a charcoal barbecue, preheat a gas barbecue to high, or preheat the grill.

2 If using *ciabatta,* slice it crossways into 4–6 pieces, then cut each piece in half horizontally. Place the bread on the grill rack or on a baking sheet. Toast, turning once, until golden brown on both sides, about 2 minutes on each side.

3 While the slices of toast are still warm, rub them on one side with the cut sides of the garlic halves, if using. Cut each tomato in half. Rub the cut sides of the tomato halves over the slices of toast until only the skins are left, then discard the skins. Drizzle with olive oil and sprinkle with salt to taste. If using sliced sourdough bread, cut the slices of toast in half. Pile up all the toasts on a serving dish or in a shallow bowl and serve.

Serve with a young, robust, slightly chilled red wine from the Penedès.

1 *ciabatta* or 8 slices coarse white bread, preferably sourdough, about 225 g (8 oz) total weight

4 cloves garlic, halved (optional)

4 small, ripe tomatoes, about 140 g (5 oz) total weight

Extra virgin olive oil for drizzling

Salt

Makes 4 servings

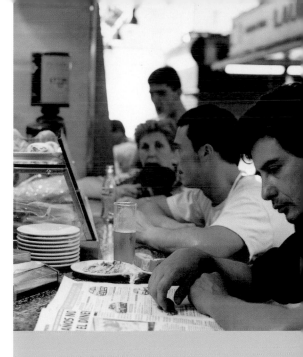

Pa amb Tomàquet

The custom of rubbing bread or toast with tomato and dressing it with olive oil and salt lies close to the heart of the Catalan way of life. *Pa amb tomàquet,* literally "bread with tomato", has clear links with other Mediterranean snacks, particularly Italian bruschetta. But the Catalans' passion for this simple food is unrivalled. *Pa amb tomàquet* is often the first thing to be brought to the table. It is a classic accompaniment to barbecued meat and fish. Along with ham, cheese, and pickles, it is sometimes eaten as a meal in itself. In fact, it is quite common for a basket of toasted bread, a bowl of tomatoes, and a bottle of oil to be placed on the table for guests to make their own.

When the Catalan food magazine *Descobrir Cuina* asked famous Catalan chefs to come up with their own versions of *pa amb tomàquet,* the results revealed their personal style. Carles Gaig placed fresh tomato pulp in a cone of crispy toast; Carme Ruscalleda combined bread and tomato in a single spoonful; and Ferran Adrià created a tomato ice cream with a wafer-thin bubble of pastry.

COCA DE RECAPTE

Flatbread with Aubergines, Sweet Peppers, and Olives

Barcelona's pastisseries don't just serve sweets. There are always a few savoury snacks to take away – usually a tasty coca *baked on the premises, with a topping of aubergine and sweet peppers, onions and raisins, spinach and pine nuts, salt anchovies, or wild mushrooms and herbs. The* coca *is described as being the Catalan version of a pizza, with a base of thin, baked crust, though the topping rarely includes cheese and only occasionally features tomato. Sweet* coques *are also made for festivals and celebrations. This recipe is the version of a savoury* coca *most often seen in Barcelona's patisseries.*

1 red sweet pepper

1 green sweet pepper

1 large aubergine

FOR THE DOUGH

265 g (8½ oz) plain flour

½ teaspoon salt

2 teaspoons baking powder

½ tablespoon olive oil

1 egg yolk

180 ml (6 fl oz) water

1 clove garlic, crushed

12 black olives, stoned and coarsely chopped

Salt and freshly ground pepper

2 large, ripe tomatoes, cut into thin slices

4 tablespoons olive oil

Makes one 30-by-23 cm (12-by-9-inch) *coca,* or 6 servings

1 Preheat the oven to 230°C (450°F). Place the sweet peppers and aubergine on a baking sheet and roast, turning several times to cook evenly, until the peppers are blistered and blackened all over and the skin of the aubergine is wrinkled and shrivelled, about 45 minutes. Transfer the peppers and aubergine to a paper bag. Close the bag and set aside until the contents are cool enough to handle, about 15 minutes. Leave the oven on.

2 Peel the charred skins from the roasted vegetables. Slice each pepper in half lengthways and discard the seeds, ribs, and stems. Cut the peppers and aubergine into thin strips.

3 While the vegetables are cooling, make the *coca* dough. Sift the flour, salt, and baking powder into a bowl. Make a well in the centre and add the olive oil and egg yolk. Gradually add the water, mixing the wet ingredients into the flour little by little using a wooden spoon. Knead the dough on a lightly floured board until soft, smooth, and elastic, about 1 minute. Form

the dough into a ball and place in a large, lightly oiled bowl. Cover with a damp tea towel and leave in a warm place until the dough puffs slightly, about 30 minutes.

4 In another large bowl, combine the aubergine and pepper strips with the garlic and olives and season generously with salt and pepper.

5 Lightly oil a 30 x 23 cm (12 x 9 inch) rimmed baking sheet. On a lightly floured work surface, roll out the dough into a rectangle to fit the tin. Press into the prepared tin and trim away any excess dough.

6 Cover the dough base with the tomato slices. Drizzle 2 tablespoons of the olive oil over the tomato slices. Arrange the aubergine mixture evenly over the tomatoes and drizzle with the remaining oil.

7 Bake the *coca* until the edges are beginning to brown, about 25 minutes. Remove from the oven and let cool slightly. Cut into squares and serve warm.

Serve with a smooth, fruity Rioja.

ENTREPANS AMB FORMATGE FRESC, ANXOVES I PEBROT

Sandwiches with Fresh Cheese, Anchovies, and Roasted Sweet Peppers

Snacks and appetisers such as tapas have always been a vital element of the Catalan way of life. The bocadillo *is the Spanish sandwich, a giant hunk of bread stuffed with ham, salchichón,* chorizo, *cheese, deep-fried squid rings, or whatever else takes your fancy. In Barcelona, the* bocadillo *is called an* entrepà, *literally "between bread", and a host of "fast-food' joints have sprung up to cater to its enormous popularity. Entrepans are eaten any time of the day, but especially in late morning, late afternoon, and late at night.*

1 Preheat the oven to 450°F (230°C). Place the sweet peppers on a baking sheet and roast them, turning several times to cook evenly, until the skins are blistered and blackened all over, about 45 minutes. Transfer the peppers to a paper bag. Close the bag and let the peppers steam until cool enough to handle, about 15 minutes. Peel off the charred skins. Slice each pepper in half lengthways and discard the seeds, ribs, and stems. Cut the peppers into strips and set aside. (The roasted peppers will keep for up to a week in the refrigerator if covered with olive oil.)

2 Preheat the grill. Slice each length of baguette in half horizontally. Transfer the baguette halves, cut side up, to a baking sheet and lightly toast under the grill for about 1 minute. Slice each tomato in half. Rub the cut sides of the tomato halves on the toasted baguette surfaces until only the skins are left, then discard the skins. Drizzle with olive oil and sprinkle with salt to taste.

3 Divide the cheese slices evenly among the bottom halves of the baguette lengths, followed by the roasted pepper strips and the anchovies. Cover each with the top halves of the baguette lengths and press gently to secure the filling. Cut each sandwich in half again, if desired, and serve at once.

Serve with a glass of ice-cold San Miguel beer.

2 large red sweet peppers

2 baguettes, cut into 15 cm (6 inch) lengths

4 small ripe tomatoes

Extra virgin olive oil for drizzling

Sea salt

4 slices fresh goat's or cow's milk cheese such as queso fresco de Burgos, each 6 mm (¼ inch) thick

8 canned anchovy fillets in olive oil

Makes 4 sandwiches

Anchovies

The little port town of L'Escala on the northern Costa Brava is to anchovies what Palamós is to prawns (page 95). L'Escala is both the capital of the catch and a byword for high quality. The anchovies are fished at night, brought into harbour in the morning, and then auctioned at the fish market to local companies. The main brands are Callol i Serrats, Casa Bordas, Soles, El Xillu, and Magdalena Sureda (the last is filleted and cured in salt). They are then sold ready for use in olive oil or preserved in salt. Salt-packed anchovies are considered to be of superior quality, but they should be rinsed of excess salt and marinated in olive oil before use.

Anxoves de L'Escala are acknowledged throughout Spain as the finest preserved anchovies on the market, and it's not hard to see why. Experiencing these fat juicy, delicious fish is a revelation. L'Escala anchovies lend themselves to a variety of culinary uses, from *coca* toppings to salads, but the best way to enjoy them is *au naturel,* on a slice of toasted country bread that has been liberally coated with olive oil and topped with a tomato slice.

PANELLETS DE PINYONS
Almond and Pine Nut Biscuits

The first day of November is All Saints' Day, and Barcelona celebrates it with special foods. Roasted chestnuts and baked sweet potatoes are sold at street stalls. Queues form in the pastisseries for one of the city's greatest delicacies, little, round almond cookies that are similar to macaroons. Classic panellets are sweetened ground almonds bound together in a dough. This is the original version, encrusted with pine nuts. Nowadays, the dough may be flavoured with a range of ingredients, from whisky to marrons glacés, and may be coated with coconut, chocolate, marzipan, or a variety of nuts.

1 small russet potato, about 125 g (¼ lb), peeled

450 g (1 lb) blanched almonds

Finely grated zest of ½ lemon

2 cups 450 g (1 lb) sugar

250 ml (8 fl oz) water

1 large egg white

75 g (2½ oz) pine nuts

Makes about 20 biscuits

1 Bring a small saucepan three-quarters full of water to a boil. Add the potato and cook until tender when pierced with a knife, about 10 minutes. Drain and transfer to a small bowl. Mash with a fork and set aside to cool slightly.

2 In a food processor, finely grind the almonds. Transfer the ground almonds to a bowl. Add the mashed potato and lemon zest and mix thoroughly.

3 In a small, heavy-bottomed saucepan, stir together the sugar and water until the sugar is dissolved. Bring to a boil over high heat, stirring with a wooden spoon until the mixture thickens to a syrup, then stop stirring. Continue cooking until the syrup registers 120°C (250°F) on a sugar thermometer (the hard-ball stage), then remove from the heat.

4 Pour the syrup in a thin stream over the almond mixture, mixing well with the wooden spoon. (Be careful at this point, as the dough will be too hot to handle.) Let cool for at least 15 minutes. Form the dough into a ball, place it in a covered bowl, or wrap in cling film and refrigerate overnight.

5 Preheat the oven to 245°C (475°F). Butter a baking sheet.

6 In a small bowl, lightly beat the egg white. Using your hands, shape the dough into balls about the size of a small walnut. Roll each ball in the egg white and then in the pine nuts, pushing the nuts slightly into the surface so they don't fall out during baking. As the balls are formed, place them about 5 cm (2 inches) apart on the prepared baking sheet.

7 Bake the biscuits until they are golden brown, 15–20 minutes. Let cool on the pan on a wire rack. Store in an airtight container for up to 1 week.

Serve with coffee after lunch or in the afternoon with a cup of tea or a glass of *moscatel*.

PA DE FETGE

Country-style Pâté

This pâté originated in the mountainous landscapes of the Cerdanya region but has since migrated south to Barcelona. Traditionally, it is wrapped in pig's caul, the delicate lacy fat surrounding the pig's stomach, and baked; hence the name, which means "liver bread". It is the Barcelonan equivalent of the British caul-wrapped sausages called "faggots". Caul is very hard to find nowadays in butchers as it is used as pet food. Serve the pâté with salad greens, toasted walnuts, pickled cucumbers, and warm toast.

1 In a bowl, soak the bread in the milk for 2 minutes. Squeeze out the milk, then grind the bread.

2 In a large bowl, combine the pork liver, pork fillet, and *panceta*. Add the eggs, bread, cognac, parsley, garlic, pimentón, cinnamon, coriander, thyme, 1 heaped teaspoon salt, and a little pepper. Mix everything together thoroughly.

3 Preheat the oven to 220°C (425°F). Line a 1 l (1¾ pint) terrine with the bacon rashers, laying them across the mould and letting the ends hang over the sides, or line the terrine with the caul. Spoon in the pâté mixture, pressing down gently to prevent air bubbles from forming. Fold the bacon or caul over the pâté.

4 Place the terrine in a baking pan and add boiling water to reach halfway up the sides of the mould. Bake, uncovered, until the top begins to brown, about 45 minutes. Cover and continue to bake until cooked through, about 45 minutes longer. Let cool completely.

5 To make the pâté compact and easily sliceable, cut a piece of cardboard to fit inside the dish and wrap it in aluminium foil. Place it on the surface of the pâté and place a heavy weight on top. Transfer to the refrigerator to chill for at least 12 hours or up to 24 hours.

6 To serve, remove the weight and cardboard and turn the pâté out on to a serving dish. If the pâté won't come out of the terrine, warm the base in a bowl of hot water, and try again. Slice and serve.

Serve with an elegant Chardonnay from the Penedès.

2 slices coarse country white bread, about 60 g (2 oz) total weight, crusts removed

120 ml (4 fl oz) whole milk

7 oz (200 g) pork liver, trimmed and finely chopped

285 g (10 oz) pork fillet, finely chopped

400 g (14 oz) *panceta* or green bacon, rind removed, finely chopped

3 large eggs, beaten

1 tablespoon good-quality cognac

Generous handful of fresh flat-leaved parsley leaves, finely chopped

4 cloves garlic, finely chopped

1 teaspoon pimentón or sweet paprika

1 teaspoon ground cinnamon

1 teaspoon ground coriander

1 teaspoon fresh thyme leaves

Salt and freshly ground pepper

16 thin bacon rashers, rinds removed, or 1 pig's caul

Makes 8 servings

French Influences

It would be surprising if neighbouring France had not had some influence on the Catalan kitchen. The onion soup of the Pyrenees is clearly borrowed from French cuisine, and the *pa de fetge* of the Cerdanya is in essence a classic French *pâté de campagne*. There is even a suggestion that the name of the traditional Catalan salad, *xató*, comes from the French word *château*. Nowadays, however, while French cooking is still highly respected, it has lost some ground to the increasingly exciting new Spanish cuisine. During the nineteenth and early twentieth centuries, when bourgeois French cuisine was at its apogee, Barcelona was proud to possess an elegant French establishment such as Le Grand Restaurant de France. Today, French chefs, such as Jean-Louis Neichel and Jean Luc Figueras, still work in Barcelona, but the tables have turned. "The great Catalan cooks of today have emancipated themselves, and while they are grateful for services rendered, they are now saying farewell to France and proposing new…Mediterranean and Catalan pleasures", writes Barcelona food critic Jaume Fàbrega.

EMPANADA DE PEBROTS I TONYINA
Sweet Pepper and Tuna Pie

Barcelona is a glorious melting pot of cultures. Waves of immigration starting in the mid-twentieth century included regional migrations such as the Galicians. In the Raval neighbourhood near the Ramblas, many Galician-owned bars are still functioning as they did in the 1950s, serving up traditional menus such as octopus salad, boiled pork, sweet almond tarta de Santiago, and bowls of Ribeiro wine. Empanadas are a favourite Galician-inspired snack that can be bought at patisseries all over the city. These squares of pastry hold various fillings, such as this tuna and sweet pepper combination, or spinach, raisins, and pine nuts.

FOR THE DOUGH

450 g (1 lb) plain flour

1 large egg

60 ml (2 fl oz) olive oil

4 tablespoons chilled unsalted butter, cut into 6 mm (¼ inch) pieces

½ teaspoon salt

4 teaspoons baking powder

120 ml (4 fl oz) full cream milk

FOR THE FILLING

60 ml (2 fl oz) olive oil

1 large yellow onion, finely chopped

2 red sweet peppers, seeded and finely chopped

6 small, ripe tomatoes, about 675 g (1½ lb) total weight, cored

285 g (10 oz) canned tuna in olive oil, drained

3 hard-boiled eggs

Leaves from 3 or 4 fresh flat-leaved parsley sprigs, finely chopped

Salt and freshly ground pepper

Milk for brushing

Makes 8 servings

1 To make the dough, sift the flour into a large bowl. Make a well in the flour and break the egg into it. Beat the egg lightly in the well, then add the olive oil, butter, salt, and baking powder. Work the liquids into the flour with your fingertips. Add the milk and mix with your hands until the dough pulls together, adding a little more milk if needed. Knead until the dough is smooth and elastic, about 1 minute. Form into a ball, cover with a clean tea towel, and refrigerate for at least 30 minutes or up to 1 hour.

2 Meanwhile, make the filling. In a large frying pan over medium heat, warm the olive oil. Add the onion and peppers and fry until the onion has softened and taken on a deep golden colour from the peppers, about 5 minutes. Cut the tomatoes in half and, using the large holes of a grater, grate the pulp directly into the pan. Discard the skins. Sauté until the tomato darkens in colour, about 5 minutes. Using a fork, flake the drained tuna into large chunks, then add to the tomato mixture. Peel and chop the eggs. Add the eggs and parsley to the pan and season to taste with salt and pepper. Cook gently until the mixture is heated through but still moist, about 5 minutes.

3 Preheat the oven to 200°C (400°F). Lightly oil a large baking sheet.

4 Divide the dough into 2 pieces, 1 piece slightly larger than the other. On a lightly floured work surface, roll out the smaller piece with a rolling pin into a 25 to 30 cm (10 to 12 inch) square. Trim and patch the dough if necessary. Place the square of dough on the prepared baking sheet.

5 Spoon the filling over the dough in an even layer, leaving a 2.5 cm (1 inch) border uncovered around the edge. Use a pastry brush to brush the edges of the dough with milk.

6 Roll out the remaining piece of dough into a square slightly larger than the first square. Carefully lay it on top of the filling and gently press the edges together with your fingers. Roll the edges inwards, towards the centre of the pie, to seal and form a narrow rim. Brush all over with milk; this will give the crust a shiny, golden surface. (If desired, a decoration of leaves or other shapes can be made with any remaining dough. Press the shapes on to the top crust and brush with milk.)

7 Bake until golden, 30–35 minutes. Serve warm or cold, cut into squares.

Serve with a light, cold Spanish beer such as San Miguel or a fragrant white Albariño wine from Galicia.

VARIANTES

Spicy Marinated Olives with Pickled Vegetables and Garlic

This bar-top snack is commonly served in Barcelona with a midday aperitif. A memorable version is offered at the Bar Mendizábal in Carrer Hospital, a small kiosk decorated in bright 1970s colours, with a miniature terrace. In Spain, variantes *are normally bought already mixed at market stalls specialising in olives and pickles, but they can easily be made at home. Briefly boiling the garlic cloves takes away some of their strong flavour, while giving them a sweet crunchiness. Any olive variety will do, although Spanish olives would be more authentic.*

1 Bring a small saucepan three-quarters full of water to a boil over high heat. Add the garlic, return to the boil, and cook for 3 minutes. Add the carrot, return again to the boil, and cook for 1 minute longer. Drain, then plunge the garlic and carrot slices into cold water. Drain again and peel the garlic (the skins can now be removed easily).

2 Transfer the garlic and carrot slices to a glass bowl. Add the olives, onions, and gherkins and mix well. Add the olive oil, vinegar, ½ teaspoon salt, chilli powder, pimentón, and thyme and stir gently to coat all the ingredients evenly. Cover and refrigerate the olive and vegetable mixture until well chilled, at least 2 hours or up to 6 hours, mixing once or twice.

Serve with a strongly flavoured aperitif such as vermouth or Campari and soda.

12 cloves garlic, unpeeled

1 carrot, peeled and cut on the diagonal into slices 6 mm (¼ inch) thick

24 mixed, brine-cured green and black olives, drained

12 cocktail onions in vinegar, drained

12 baby gherkins in vinegar, drained

2 tablespoons extra-virgin olive oil

1 tablespoon white wine vinegar

Salt

Pinch of chilli powder

½ teaspoon pimentón (smoked paprika) or sweet paprika

Generous pinch of fresh thyme leaves

Makes 4 servings

Aperitiu

The pre-luncheon drink is a sacred element of Spanish social life. On any given day, friends meet midday over an ice-cold beer, a small tumbler of vermouth or a glass of wine. While the *aperitiu* (aperitif) is very much alive as a custom, its nature is changing. In the old days, the classic drink was vermouth, from a barrel or on tap. But this is now the province of the elderly, which is a shame, because Barcelona has some fine local examples of *vermut*. Nowadays, the drinks of choice are red wine by the glass for the discerning minority, and beer for the majority. The *canya* is a 250 ml (8 fl oz) glass of beer from the tap; if you ask for *una cerveza,* it will probably come in a bottle. The *cerveseria,* or "beer hall", is a relatively new concept imported from Madrid, offering tapas or *raciones* (larger servings of tapas) along with beer on tap. San Miguel, the best-known Spanish brewery, is based in Lleida. Other common brands are Cruzcampo, Estrella Damm, Aguila, and Mahou. An interest in *cerveza dorada,* dark beer, is growing in Barcelona; it is served in bars such as Xampanyet and Quimet i Quimet.

ESCABETX DE SARDINES
Fried Sardines in Vinaigrette

Escabetx, or pickling in vinegar and spices, is one of the oldest means of preserving food. Partridges and pigeons en escabetx were common sights at the banqueting tables of medieval Catalonia. Ruperto de Nola's sixteenth-century cookery book, Llibre del Coch, gives recipes for escabetxos of rabbit, aubergine and sturgeon. The technique has persisted in contemporary Spanish cuisine, and these days cold escabetxos appear from time to time on the menu at Barcelona's elegant tapas bars. Although originally used for meat and game, the preparation works well with any oily, strong-flavoured fish.

1 kg (2¼ lb) fresh sardines, filleted

285 g (10 oz) plain flour

Salt and freshly ground pepper

Equal parts olive and sunflower oil for frying

90 ml (3 fl oz) olive oil

2 bay leaves

12 peppercorns

3 cloves garlic, crushed

1 teaspoon pimentón (smoked paprika) or sweet paprika

250 ml (8 fl oz) white wine vinegar

Makes 6 servings

1 If your fishmonger has not done so, first prepare the sardines. Hold a sardine by the tail, letting it hang down into a sink full of water, and scrape the scales from the fish by rubbing them off with your fingertips or using the blunt edge of a knife blade, starting at the tail end and working down towards the head (the scales will fly in all directions). Rinse well. Clean each fish by snapping off the head and cutting into the cavity on the belly side, from the anal vent up to the head. Run your thumb along the belly to open, then remove and discard the entrails. Using your fingers, loosen the backbone near the tail end and pull it out along with as many of its fine lateral bones as possible, working towards the head, so the fish forms a single flat fillet. Rinse thoroughly and let drain.

2 Place the flour on a plate or in a shallow bowl, season it with salt and pepper, and stir to combine. Toss the sardines in the seasoned flour to coat lightly, shaking off any excess.

3 Pour the olive and sunflower oils to a depth of 2.5 cm (1 inch) into a large, heavy-bottomed frying pan and heat over high heat until smoking hot. In batches, add the sardines and fry them, turning once, until golden brown, about 2 minutes on each side. As the sardines finish cooking, transfer them to a *cassola* or clay casserole. When all the sardines are cooked, sprinkle with salt and set aside.

4 Clean the frying pan and add the 6 tablespoons olive oil. Warm the oil over medium heat until hot. Add the bay leaves, peppercorns, and garlic and fry until the garlic is lightly browned, about 3 minutes. Remove from the heat, add the pimentón, and stir once or twice to combine. Add the vinegar and 250 ml (8 fl oz) water, return to medium heat, and simmer until reduced by a quarter, about 5 minutes.

5 Pour the contents of the frying pan over the sardines and shake the *cassola* a little to ensure that the vinegar mixture is evenly distributed. Set aside and leave to cool. The sardines can be served at once, but will taste better after a day or two in the refrigerator, tightly covered, where they will keep for up to 5 days. Bring to room temperature before serving.

Serve with a chilled, very dry *fino* sherry.

AIRE
ACONDICIONADO

COCA DE VIDRE

Sweet Pastry with Pine Nuts

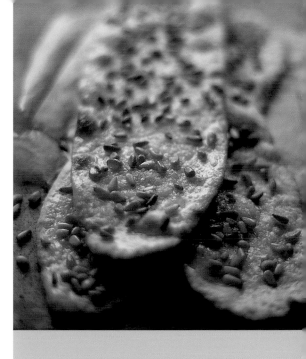

Coca de vidre is a thin sheet of pastry flavoured with aniseed liqueur and pine nuts and caramelised with sugar until it is hard and crunchy; hence the name, which translates as "glass coca". You can buy coca at stalls such as the one outside the cinema at Maremagnum, the giant mall down by the old harbour where all of Barcelona seems to convene on Sunday afternoons to go to the cinema. The long, thin board of crisp pastry crumbles into shards as you bite into it, showering the pavement with sugary crumbs.

1 To make the dough, sift the flour into a large bowl. Add the baking powder and whisk to combine. Add the milk, salt, sugar, olive oil, and 1 teaspoon aniseed liqueur. Mix with your hands into a smooth elastic dough. Form into a ball, cover with a clean tea towel, and let rest for 20 minutes.

2 Preheat the oven to 220°C (425°F). Butter 2 large baking sheets.

3 Cut the dough into 4 equal pieces. Pull each piece into a thick sausage shape. On a lightly floured surface, roll out each piece of dough until it is as thin as possible (about 3 mm/⅛ inch thick), yet still easy to handle. It should be roughly three times as long as it is wide and have rounded ends. Carefully transfer to a prepared baking sheet. Repeat with the remaining dough pieces.

4 Prick the surface of each pastry all over with a fork and brush the pastries with the 2 tablespoons olive oil. Sprinkle evenly with the pine nuts and the sugar. Bake until golden brown, about 15 minutes. As soon as the pastries emerge from the oven, drizzle them evenly with the anise liqueur. Serve warm or at room temperature.

Serve with a glass of semi-sweet sparkling *cava*.

FOR THE DOUGH

450 g (1 lb) plain flour

1 teaspoon baking powder

375 ml (12 fl oz) full-cream milk

1 teaspoon salt

1 tablespoon sugar

2 tablespoons extra virgin olive oil

1 teaspoon aniseeed liqueur such as *anis seco*, Pernod, or pastis

FOR THE TOPPING

2 tablespoons extra virgin olive oil

115 g (4 oz) pine nuts

115 g (4 oz) sugar

120 ml (4 fl oz) anise liqueur such as *anis seco*, Pernod, or pastis

Makes 4 pastries, or 8 servings

Sweet Snacks

An entire category of sweet Catalan foods exists that are not eaten as pudding but as snacks, "per picar", as they say in Barcelona. Some are closely associated with a place or time of year: *coca de Sant Joan, mona de Pasqua* (page 174), and *tortell de Reis,* for example, are made exclusively for certain religious festivals. *Turrón* (nougat) is eaten at Christmas, and *panellets* (pine nut cookies; page 80), *orelletes* (deep-fried pastry "ears"), and *bunyols* (anise-flavoured doughnuts) are much loved fiesta foods.

Even if they have no direct festive link, there is something about these sweets that makes them special and celebratory. *Carquinyolis* (almond cookies) are often dunked in *moscatel* for a luxurious snack. *Dulce de membrillo* (quince paste) is a Spanish favourite often served with cheese but equally delicious on its own. *Pastissets de Tortosa,* little pies stuffed with shredded pumpkin, make a delicious breakfast with a big cup of *café con leche.* And a range of sweet *coques,* including *coques de llardons* (sweet pastry with pork scratchings; page 65), are favourite afternoon snacks.

CROQUETES DE POLLASTRE I PERNIL
Chicken and Ham Croquettes

There is no point in pretending there is anything authentically Catalan about this dish. Croquetas (croquetes in Catalan) belong in the repertoire of every Spanish housewife, whether in Barcelona or Burgos. The dish has its roots in the economical cooking of a less prosperous time in Europe, when meat was a luxury and to throw away leftovers was unthinkable. In Catalonia, as elsewhere, the remains of Sunday lunch would find their way into croquetes on Monday. Nowadays, these fried morsels are on the menu of nearly every tapas bar in Barcelona. They make a tasty snack at midday or a comforting addition to supper.

3 tablespoons olive oil, plus more for frying

3 tablespoons plain flour

360 ml (12 fl oz) full cream milk

360 ml (12 fl oz) chicken stock

60 g (2 oz) cooked chicken meat, minced

60 g (2 oz) serrano or other dry salted ham, finely chopped

Pinch of freshly grated nutmeg

Salt and freshly ground pepper

115 g (4 oz) fine dry breadcrumbs

2 large eggs, beaten

Makes about 20 croquettes, or 5 servings

1 In a small, heavy-bottomed saucepan over low heat, combine the 3 tablespoons olive oil and the flour. Cook, stirring constantly, until the flour has absorbed all the oil, 2–3 minutes. Add the milk and stock, little by little, stirring constantly with a wooden spoon. Use a whisk to smooth out the sauce if lumps start to form. Cook the sauce, continuing to stir constantly, until smooth and thick, 10–15 minutes. Remove from the heat, stir in the chicken, ham, and nutmeg and season to taste with salt and pepper.

2 Pour the mixture into a metal baking tin and let cool to room temperature. Cover with cling film and refrigerate the mixture overnight. By the next day, the mixture will have congealed into a thick paste.

3 Put the breadcrumbs in a shallow bowl, and lightly beat the eggs in a second shallow bowl. Using a spoon and your hands, form the chilled paste into short logs 2 inches (5 cm) long and about 1 inch (2.5 cm) in diameter. Roll them once in the breadcrumbs, then in the beaten eggs, and then again in the breadcrumbs, making sure each croquette is thoroughly coated.

4 Pour olive oil to a depth of 2.5 cm (1 inch) into a large frying pan and heat over medium-high heat until very hot. Slip in the croquettes a few at a time and fry, turning once, until golden brown, about 3 minutes. Transfer to a plate lined with paper towels to drain. Serve at once.

Serve with a robust and plummy Cabernet Sauvignon from Madrid.

GAMBES A LA PLANXA
Griddled Prawns with Garlic and Parsley

Griddled prawns are a fixture on the menu, along with paella and barbecued fish, at nearly every beach restaurant up and down the Mediterranean coast from the Costa Brava to Alicante. La planxa (plancha in Spanish), a kind of griddle, is arguably the Spanish cook's favourite cooking tool. At its most basic, it is a metal surface that can be heated from below, preferably over an open fire. It has an important advantage over a conventional barbecue: the juices from whatever is being cooked are retained and concentrated and never drip into the fire.

1 Season the prawns with salt and pepper and drizzle generously with olive oil.

2 Place a griddle or a large frying pan over high heat until hot. The griddle is ready when a drop of water flicked on the surface sizzles and evaporates instantly. Place the prawns on the hot surface and cook, turning once, until they are opaque throughout and the shells begin to brown, about 5 minutes on each side. Sprinkle the garlic and parsley over the prawns; cook, without stirring, for about 30 seconds; and then turn the prawns one last time. Transfer to a warmed serving dish and serve at once.

Serve with a crisp, acidic white wine with a slight sparkle, such as Vi d'Agulla from the Empordà.

24 large fresh prawns on the shell, about 675 g (1½ lb) total weight

Salt and freshly ground pepper

Olive oil for drizzling

4 cloves garlic, finely chopped

Handful of fresh flat-leaved parsley leaves, finely chopped

Makes 4 servings

Prawns

Prawns are fished at several points along the Spanish coast, but the best prawns of all, according to the Catalans, are caught by the fishermen of Palamós, a seaport on the Costa Brava. The famous *gambes de Palamós* spend their lives in undersea trenches 250 to 800 m (800 to 2,600 feet) deep. They are caught with dredging nets, brought into the harbour, and washed clean, after which their characteristic intense red colour begins to show. (They are known locally as "the red miracle"). Seared briefly *a la planxa* with sea salt and olive oil, these prawns have a creamy, almost buttery texture and a wonderfully rich, concentrated taste. The fame of the *gamba* has spread far and wide, while, sadly, the creature itself has become progressively scarcer. Once it was common for a fisherman to bring in over 100 kg (200 lb) a day; today the catch has fallen to an average of 20 kg (40 lb) or less. Demand therefore outstrips supply, and prices have soared, making the Palamós prawn one of Catalonia's most expensive seafoods.

ENTRANTS

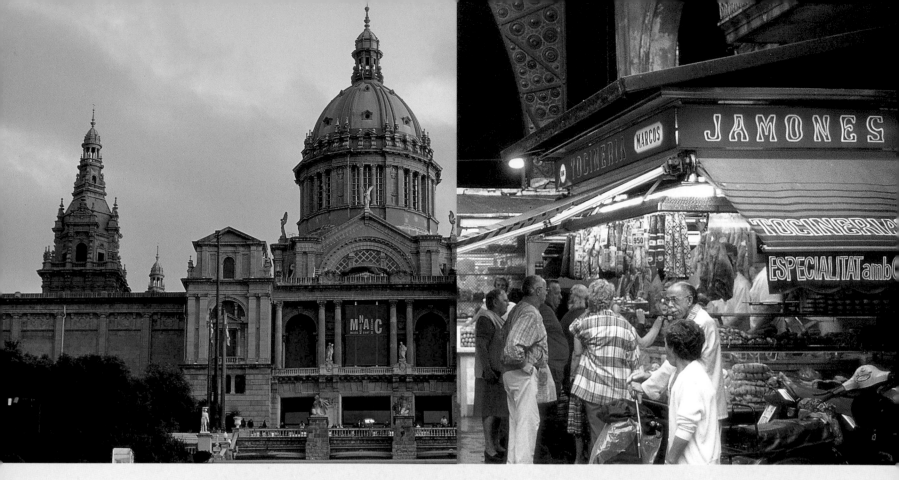

From baked autumn mushrooms and hearty spring vegetable and

garlic soup to fresh summer salads, *entrants* are driven by the seasons.

The typical concept of a first course is a dish that is light, usually a soup or salad. But in Catalan cooking and in Spanish food in general, first courses, although served in small portions, are often rich and filling. Because many favourite *entrants* share the heft and appeal of a main course, dishes such as stuffed cabbage leaves or broad beans with spare ribs and sausage *(faves a la catalana)* may be offered as either a first course or as a second course with a salad. By the same token, it is not unusual to forgo the second course and make a meal of *entrants* – for example, on a hot day, when cold gazpacho and country bread are called for.

GASPATXO ANDALÚS

Gazpacho

Barcelona may be the capital of Catalonia, but it is also a dynamic culinary melting pot in which other Spanish regions are well represented. In April, the Andalusian community of Barcelona, the city's largest minority group at one million strong, holds its own version of Seville's famous spring fair. All the ingredients are there – frilly dresses, folk dancing, and fino *sherry in vast quantities. As you feast on typical southern foods such as* pescaíto frito *(fried fish) and gazpacho, you have to pinch yourself to remember you're not in Andalusia.*

1 Place 9 slices of the bread in a food processor and spoon the vinegar over them. Then add the tomatoes, onion, cucumber, and pepper chunks, 150 ml (5 fl oz) of the olive oil, and 250 ml (8 fl oz) water and pulse until smooth. Add more water if desired – some people like their gazpacho thick, while others prefer a runnier consistency – and pulse again. Season to taste with salt and more vinegar, if desired.

2 Cover and refrigerate until well chilled, at least 2 hours or up to 4 hours.

3 Meanwhile, cut the remaining 2 bread slices into 12 mm (½ inch) cubes. In a frying pan over medium-high heat, warm the remaining 90 ml (3 fl oz) olive oil. Add the bread cubes and fry, stirring often, until golden brown on all sides, about 3 minutes. Transfer to paper towels to drain.

4 Just before serving, transfer the gazpacho to a serving bowl and add the ice cubes. Place the diced cucumber, diced pepper, hard-boiled eggs, ham, and prepared bread cubes in individual small bowls to serve as garnishes. Pass the bowls at the table for guests to top their soup as desired.

Serve with a crisp, light white wine from southern Spain.

11 slices day-old coarse country white bread, about 285 g (10 oz) total weight, crusts removed

2 tablespoons sherry vinegar, or to taste

1.5 kg (3 lb) ripe tomatoes, peeled and seeded (page 187)

½ yellow onion, cut into chunks

1 small cucumber, peeled, halved, seeded, and cut into chunks

1 red sweet pepper, seeded and cut into chunks

250 ml (8 fl oz) extra virgin olive oil

Sea salt

Handful of ice cubes

FOR THE GARNISH

1 small cucumber, peeled, halved, seeded, and diced

1 red sweet pepper, seeded and diced

2 hard-boiled eggs, peeled and chopped

2 slices serrano ham, finely chopped

Makes 6–8 servings

Spanish Regional Influences

In a globalised world, it is increasingly difficult to draw fixed boundaries around national cuisines. More and more, the influences from outside determine the development of a particular cuisine. Catalan cooking, like Catalonia itself, has always been open to the cultural currents of a wider world, and now more so than ever. The influences are coming not just from Asia, South America, and Africa, however, but from the rest of Spain as well. Although tapas, the famed little dishes made for snacking with drinks, originated in southern Spain, they were never part of Catalan life. Yet they are steadily becoming more popular in Barcelona, which now boasts a number of Madrid-style tapas bars. The Basque *pintxo,* a kind of canapé served on trays at Basque bars, is gaining wider acceptance, too. Andalusian and Galician dishes such as gazpacho, *pulpo a la gallega* (marinated octopus), and empanadas are also regular fixtures on local menus. All these influences contribute to the rich and varied mixture that makes up Barcelona's food scene.

ALBERGINIES FARCIDES
Stuffed Aubergines

Glossy purple-black aubergines at peak season in Barcelona are so fresh they give off a sweet, sun-ripened aroma. Catalan cuisine has a number of uses for them. They can be stewed with sweet peppers and tomatoes for samfaina *(page 141) or grilled for* escalivada *(page 118). In Majorca, they are made into fritters and served drizzled with honey. Perhaps best of all, they can be stuffed and baked in the oven. This recipe originates from the Balearic Islands, but it is now a favourite in Barcelona where it makes regular appearances on menus – especially during aubergine season.*

3 small aubergines, about 175 g (6 oz) each

Salt and freshly ground pepper

5 tablespoons olive oil

1 yellow onion, finely chopped

6 cloves garlic, finely chopped

225 g (8 oz) minced pork

225 g (8 oz) minced veal

4 large, ripe tomatoes, about 450 g (1 lb) total weight, peeled, seeded (page 187), and finely chopped

2 fresh marjoram or oregano sprigs

1 bay leaf

120 ml (4 fl oz) single cream

90 g (3 oz) Mahón, Parmesan, or other hard cow's milk cheese, grated

Handful of fresh flat-leaved parsley leaves, finely chopped

Makes 6 servings

1 Cut the aubergines in half lengthways. Using a spoon, scoop out the flesh into a colander, leaving a shell about ½ inch (12 mm) thick. Sprinkle the shells and flesh with salt. Place the shells cut side down in a separate colander or on paper towels to drain for about 1 hour. (Salting an aubergine draws out its bitter juices.) Rinse in cold water and dry thoroughly.

2 Preheat the oven to 180°C (350°F). Select a shallow ovenproof dish in which the aubergine shells will fit, cut side up, snugly side by side (This will help them to retain their shape while cooking). Rub them all over with 1 tablespoon olive oil. Arrange in the dish and bake until soft, 15–20 minutes.

3 Meanwhile, finely chop the aubergine flesh. In a heavy-bottomed frying pan over medium heat, warm the rest of the olive oil. Add the onion and sauté until softened, about 6 minutes. Then add the garlic, chopped aubergine, pork, and veal. Cook, stirring, until the meat is nicely browned, about 10 minutes. Add the tomatoes, marjoram, and bay leaf and season to taste with salt and pepper. Continue to cook, stirring until the liquid has almost entirely evaporated, about 10 minutes longer. Discard the bay leaf.

4 Spoon the filling into the aubergine shells. Drizzle a little single cream over each and top with the cheese and parsley. If desired, sprinkle with freshly ground black pepper. Bake until the cheese is bubbling and golden brown, 25–30 minutes. Let cool slightly before serving.

Serve with a full-bodied, well-balanced red wine from the Ribera del Duero.

TREMPÓ

Majorcan Summer Salad

Historians tell us that trempó *comes from the medieval Catalan* trempar, *meaning "to dress" with salt, oil, and vinegar – a word that has died out in Catalonia proper but persists on the island of Majorca. This simple summer salad is not really worth making out of season, as the ingredients must be fully ripe and delicious – and organic if possible. This is only a basic recipe; lettuce, cucumber, olives, and even pears and apples can be added as you like. Serve with a vinaigrette or with a bowl of* allioli *on the side.*

1 To make the vinaigrette, in a bowl whisk together the vinegar and ½ teaspoon salt. Slowly add the olive oil while whisking constantly. Taste and adjust the seasoning with salt and pepper.

2 Alternatively, make the *allioli:* Using a mortar and pestle, crush together the garlic and ½ teaspoon coarse salt into a thick, smooth paste. Transfer the garlic paste to a bowl. Using a whisk and beating vigorously and continuously, add the oil drop by drop, then in a thin stream, until the sauce thickens into a golden mayonnaise, about 15 minutes. Add the lemon juice and stir to combine. To make the *allioli* in a food processor, combine the garlic and ½ teaspoon coarse salt and process to a paste. With the machine running, slowly drizzle in the oil in a thin stream until the sauce thickens. Stir in the lemon juice.

3 Place the tomatoes, spring onion, and sweet peppers in a large bowl and toss to combine. Dress the salad with the vinaigrette, toss well, and serve. Alternatively, serve the salad with a bowl of *allioli*.

Serve with a spicy, rustic red wine from Majorca.

FOR THE VINAIGRETTE

2 tablespoons red or white wine vinegar

Salt and freshly ground pepper

90 ml (3 fl oz) extra virgin olive oil

FOR THE ALLIOLI

12 cloves garlic, peeled

Coarse salt

250 ml (8 fl oz) extra virgin olive oil

1 teaspoon fresh lemon juice

FOR THE SALAD

3 large, ripe tomatoes, coarsely chopped

1 thick spring onion, including pale green parts, or 1 small yellow onion, thinly sliced

1 green sweet pepper, seeded and cut into narrow strips or rings

1 red sweet pepper, seeded and cut into narrow strips or rings

Makes 4 servings

The Balearic Islands

The islands of Majorca, Minorca, Ibiza and Formentera (in decreasing order of size) are not part of Catalonia proper but are considered to be *països catalans* (Catalan lands), and they share culinary traditions and cultures with the mainland. A combination of history and circumstance has shaped the cuisine of these islands, allowing them to preserve some of the medieval dishes that have died out in Catalonia itself, such as the *flao* of Ibiza (page 177), and the *escaldums* (a rich chicken stew) and *menjar blanc* (blancmange) of Majorca. Minorca has a number of culinary preparations that hark back to British domination in the eighteenth century, such as *grevi* (gravy) and *piquel* (pickle). According to a widely accepted theory, *maionesa* (mayonnaise) was taken back to France after the brief French occupation of the island. Many local specialities reflect the emphasis on robust foods from these islands, such as *arròs de matances,* a soupy rice and pork dish seasoned with saffron and garlic from Ibiza, or the Christmas favourite, *salsa de Nadal,* a potent mixture of almonds, chicken stock, chicken and pork fat, sugar, saffron, and spices.

SOPA D'ALL I VEGETALS DE PRIMAVERA

Garlic and Spring Vegetable Soup

Garlic soup is a staple dish of Catalan and Spanish villages. Agricultural labourers found it easy to prepare and restorative after a hard morning's harvest. The writer of an 1845 guidebook to Spain commented, "The Catalonians have a national soup, which is made of bread and garlic.... The better classes turn up their noses at these odoriferous delicacies of the peasantry". As a dish, sopa d'all is quite simple. But master chef Carme Ruscalleda, of the world-renowned Sant Pau restaurant near Barcelona, has taken this garlic soup a step further, adding spring vegetables for an extra dimension of colour and crunch.

Salt

155 g (5 oz) shelled broad beans

120 ml (4 fl oz) extra virgin olive oil

1 head garlic, cloves separated and peeled

8 slices coarse country wholemeal bread, about 225 g (½ lb) total weight, crusts removed

Generous dash of red or white wine vinegar

4 large eggs

4 large green asparagus spears, trimmed and chopped into 2.5 cm (1 inch) lengths

4 large white asparagus spears, trimmed and cut into 2.5 cm (1 inch) lengths

1 small head radicchio or curly endive, cored and cut into 2.5 cm (1 inch) dice

140 g (5 oz) shelled garden peas

Makes 4 servings

1 Unless you are using very small, young broad beans, you will need to remove the tough skins. Bring a small saucepan three-quarters full of water to a boil. Salt the water and add the broad beans. Blanch for 1–2 minutes, then drain and rinse under cold running water. Pinch each bean opposite the end where it was attached to the pod and squeeze; the bean should pop free. Set the skinned beans aside.

2 In a heavy-bottomed saucepan over medium heat, warm half the olive oil. Add the garlic and sauté until soft, about 3 minutes. Add the bread and fry until evenly browned, about 2 minutes longer. Add 1 l (1¾ pints) water and stir briefly to combine. Transfer to a blender or food processor and process until smooth. Season to taste with salt. Return to the saucepan, cover, and keep warm over low heat.

3 Bring a wide shallow saucepan pan three-quarters full of water to a boil over high heat. Add the vinegar and 1 teaspoon salt. Turn off the heat. Break an egg into a saucer and gently slide the egg into the water. Repeat with a second egg. Alternatively, cook the eggs in an egg poacher. Cover the pan and let stand until the whites are firm but the yolks are still runny, about 3 minutes. Using a slotted spoon, transfer the eggs to a bowl of ice water. Repeat with the remaining 2 eggs. Leave the eggs in the ice water until ready to use.

4 In a wide frying pan over medium heat, warm the rest of the olive oil. Add the asparagus, radicchio or curly endive, broad beans, and peas and sauté until just tender, about 6 minutes. Using a slotted spoon, transfer the vegetables to shallow soup bowls, dividing them evenly. Add a poached egg to each bowl.

5 Reheat the bread and garlic broth gently to serving temperature, if necessary. Divide evenly among the bowls and serve at once.

Serve with a velvety red wine from Valdepeñas.

XATÓ

Curly Endive Salad with Salt Cod, Anchovies, and Olives

The basis of this salad is a bed of crisp curly endive, crunchy and satisfying, combined with strips of salt cod, anchovies, tuna, and a scattering of black olives. But the true glory of xató is its sauce, a kind of romesco made with pounded or ground almonds and hazelnuts, nyora peppers, garlic, and olive oil. The genius of the dish is the way the rich, nutty sauce combines with the salty chunks of fish and the satisfying crunch of the curly endive. A loaf of crusty bread is essential to mop up the delicious sauce left at the bottom of the plate.

1 To prepare the salt cod, place it in a bowl of cold water to cover, cover the bowl, and refrigerate for 3 days, changing the water at least once a day.

2 To make the sauce, in a dry, heavy frying pan over medium heat, toast the almonds until browned, about 30 seconds. Transfer to a plate to cool. If using nyora peppers, let them soak in boiling water for 10 minutes, then scrape the flesh off the skins. Sprinkle the coarse country bread with the vinegar. Using a large mortar and pestle, grind together the almonds, hazelnuts, garlic, peppers, and the vinegar-soaked bread until a thick, reddish paste forms. Alternatively, process the ingredients together in a food processor, making sure the mixture remains coarse. Add the olive oil in a thin stream, stirring constantly with a wooden spoon, until the ingredients are thoroughly combined and the sauce is just liquid enough to be poured. Season with salt. (The sauce will keep in the refrigerator for 1 week. Use leftover sauce with roasts or vegetables.)

3 Remove any bones and skin from the salt cod, then shred the meat with your fingers into thin strips. Cut or tear the anchovy fillets into strips. Place the salt cod, anchovies, and tuna in a bowl with the tomatoes and olives and toss to combine. Add enough of the sauce to coat everything thickly and toss again.

4 Just before serving, in a large salad bowl, toss the curly endive with the salt cod mixture. Serve at once.

Serve with a fragrant, young white wine such as a Spanish Sauvignon Blanc.

175 g (6 oz) salt cod

FOR THE SAUCE

60 g (2 oz) blanched almonds

4 *nyora* or *romesco* peppers, ancho chillies, or 1 teaspoon pimentón (smoked paprika) or cayenne pepper (see page 186)

1 slice coarse country white bread, about 30 g (1 oz), crusts removed

1 tablespoon red wine vinegar

8–10 hazelnuts

4 cloves garlic, peeled

90 ml (3 fl oz) extra virgin olive oil

Salt

8 anchovy fillets

175 g (6 oz) tuna in olive oil, drained and separated into 2.5 cm (1 inch) chunks

2 ripe tomatoes, coarsely chopped

115 g (4 oz) black olives, preferably Arbequina

1 head curly endive or batavia, cored and separated into leaves

Makes 6 servings

Fiesta Foods: Xató

Catalonia has always been a food-loving land, but the recent explosion of food fiestas is nothing less than a sociological phenomenon. After the *calçolada* (see page 121) came the *pesolada* in the Maresme district, an event devoted to the humble pea and its use in dishes such as *pèsols ofegats* (braised peas). Then came the *botifarrada,* a celebration of *botifarras,* or blood puddings, and the *caracolada* and *sardinada,* celebrations of the snail and sardine, respectively. Not to be outdone, the residents of Vilanova i la Geltrú, Sitges, Cunit, and Vendrell, centres of the dish *xató,* decided to put on their own show, and the *xatonada* was born. It has become a major event, especially at fiesta time, when towns in the coastal area south of Barcelona celebrate the salad with processions and dances. Most *xatonades* include tastings and a competition in which cooks are invited to submit their own versions.

There are now so many food-related fiestas in Catalonia that the regional government has produced the *Agenda Gastronòmica de Catalunya,* a diary which tracks them through the year.

SOPA DE RAP I FARIGOLA
Thyme Soup with Monkfish Medallions

Fresh thyme simmered in water with bread, oil, and salt – nothing more – sopa de farigola belongs to an ancient family of soups in Catalonia and Provence made with parsley, sage, mint, and other fresh herbs. To modern palates, the absence of stock might seem to make the soup seem too thin. In practice, it can be wonderfully soothing food – pure aromatherapy, as the perfumes of the herbs and olive oil gently penetrate the senses. This version of the dish, using a quick fish stock flavoured with a sofregit *of vegetables and adding medallions of monkfish, comes from Margaret Nofre of the Sant Carles restaurant in Tortosa.*

450 g (1 lb) monkfish, cod, hake, or other firm-fleshed white fish on the bone, skin and dark membrane removed by the fishmonger

60 ml (2 fl oz) extra virgin olive oil

1 large carrot, peeled and finely chopped

1 large yellow onion, finely chopped

1 large tomato, finely chopped

4 fresh thyme sprigs

Salt and freshly ground pepper

12 slices French bread or 4 slices coarse country white bread, about 115 g (4 oz) total weight

1–2 cloves garlic, halved

Makes 4 servings

1 Cut away the fish flesh from the bones, leaving a little on the bones to add flavour to the stock. Cut the fish fillet horizontally into medallions 5 cm (2 inches) in diameter and 12 mm (½ inch) thick. Set the bones and medallions aside separately.

2 Next, make a *sofregit:* In a frying pan over medium heat, warm the olive oil. Add the carrot, onion and tomato and sauté until the onion is softened and translucent, about 10 minutes. Add the monkfish bones and cook, stirring, for 2 minutes. Reduce the heat to low, add 1.25 l (2 pints) water, and cook, covered, for about 15 minutes. Add the thyme and cook for 5 minutes longer.

3 Remove from the heat and strain the stock through a fine-meshed sieve, pressing on the vegetables with a wooden spoon to extract all the liquid. Return the stock to the pan, season to taste with salt and

pepper, and add the monkfish medallions. Bring to a simmer over low heat and cook until the fish is opaque throughout, about 5 minutes.

4 Preheat the grill. Place the bread slices on a baking sheet and toast them, turning once, until lightly golden, about 2 minutes on each side. While the bread is still warm, rub it on one side with the cut sides of the garlic halves.

5 Place 3 slices of toasted French bread or 1 slice of toasted country bread in each soup bowl and divide the medallions among the bowls. Pour the stock over the fish and serve.

Serve with a fruity, full-bodied Penedès white wine, preferably made from Parellada grapes.

FAVES A LA CATALANA
Catalan-Style Broad Beans

When the first baby broad beans come into season in early spring, Barcelona's cooks pounce on them. All over the city, kitchen hands are put to work shelling the little vegetables, most of which will find their way into one of Catalonia's most celebrated dishes, a mixture of tender broad beans; morsels of pork, bacon, and sausage, and refreshing mint. It's a thoroughly traditional dish, but one that seems modern at the same time. When the beans are fresh and tiny, before the skins turn leathery, they are one of the most delectable foods in the world.

1 Unless you are using very small, young broad beans, you will need to remove their tough skins. Bring a small saucepan three-quarters full of water to a boil. Salt the water and add the broad beans. Blanch the beans for 1–2 minutes, then drain and rinse under cold running water. Pinch each bean opposite the end where it was attached to the pod and squeeze; the bean should pop free. Set the skinned beans aside.

2 In a heavy frying pan over medium heat, warm the olive oil. Add the spare ribs and *panceta* and fry until golden, about 10 minutes. Using a slotted spoon, transfer to paper towels to drain. Add the *botifarra* slices and fry until crisp on both sides, 4–5 minutes. Using the spoon, transfer to paper towels to drain.

3 Add the spring onions to the same pan and sauté until softened, about 4 minutes. Add the garlic and sauté for about 2 minutes longer. Add the broad beans, stir, and pour in the wine. Season with salt and pepper, add the herb bundle and stir to combine. Place the spare ribs and *panceta* on top of the beans. Cover, reduce the heat to low, and simmer, shaking the pan occasionally and adding more wine if the mixture dries out, until the beans are tender, 10–15 minutes.

4 Uncover and mix together with a spoon, adding the *botifarra* slices. Simmer for 1–2 minutes longer.

5 Stir the shredded mint leaves into the beans. Remove and discard the herb bundle, transfer the beans to a serving dish and serve with the bread.

Serve with a spicy white wine such as Sauvignon Blanc.

Salt and freshly ground pepper

1 kg (2¼ lb) shelled broad beans, preferably young and tender

120 ml (4 fl oz) olive oil

285 g (10 oz) pork spare ribs, cut into 2.5 cm (1 inch) pieces

6 slices *panceta* or unsmoked bacon, cut into 5 cm (2 inch) lengths

225 g (8 oz) *botifarra negra* or other blood sausage, thickly sliced

2 small spring onions, white and pale green parts, finely chopped

4 cloves garlic, finely chopped

250 ml (8 fl oz) dry white wine, or more as needed

6 fresh flat-leaved parsley sprigs, 1 bay leaf and 3 fresh mint sprigs, tied in a bundle with kitchen string

Shredded fresh mint leaves for garnish

Warm crusty bread for serving

Makes 6 servings

Spring Vegetables

Spring in Barcelona brings a host of pleasures: a stroll down the Ramblas among flower stalls stacked with blooms and birds twittering in their cages; the joyous rituals of the fiesta, when papier-mâché *gegants* (giants) totter among the laughing crowds; and, at the markets, the arrival of the first spring vegetables. The young produce is a colourful and varied bounty, with artichokes so tender they can be eaten raw (or sliced and cooked *a la planxa*); little white-and-purple turnips with bright green tops; the first asparagus from Aragón and Navarre; fresh garlic, sweet and mild enough to use with generous abandon; and, above all, the first baby beans and peas in their pods, much adored by the Catalans and celebrated in such dishes as *faves a la catalana* and *pèsols de llavaneres ofegats* (braised peas). When spring reaches the city, there's no better way to exploit its gifts than with a platter of steamed fresh vegetables, simply dressed with butter and pepper or olive oil and lemon juice. Another favourite is a vegetable paella made with quartered artichokes, broad beans, peas, asparagus, Swiss chard, baby turnips, and sliced garlic.

TRINXAT

Mashed Potatoes and Cabbage

Like many of the best Catalan dishes, this is a simple preparation. It consists of cooked cabbage and potatoes roughly mashed together and topped with fried strips of cansalada, *or cured pork fat (a delicious, salty green bacon is a good substitute).* Trinxat, *which means "mashed", is the kind of dish a farmer's wife might whip up at the end of a cold winter's day. Some say it tastes best after the first frost, which has the effect of improving the flavour of winter cabbage. Although its roots are in the Pyrenees, this dish is now found on the menus of many elegant restaurants. It is sometimes accompanied by* allioli *(page 105).*

Salt and freshly ground pepper

1 head green cabbage, about 1 lb (450 g), cored and sliced

450 g (1 lb) waxy, yellow-fleshed potatoes, cut into thick slices

½ lb (225 g) *cansalada, panceta,* or green bacon rashers

4 tablespoons olive oil

1 teaspoon pimentón (smoked paprika) or sweet paprika

1 clove garlic, finely chopped

Makes 4 servings

1 Bring a large pot three-quarters full of water to a boil over high heat. Salt the water, add the cabbage and cook until just tender, about 15 minutes. Add the potatoes and cook until tender when pierced with a knife, about 10 minutes longer. Drain the cabbage and potatoes, then transfer to a large bowl. Using a fork or a potato masher, roughly mash the cabbage and potatoes together. Transfer to a serving dish and season to taste with salt and pepper (be careful not to use too much salt – the bacon will be quite salty).

2 While the potatoes are cooking, remove the skin or rind from the *cansalada, panceta,* or bacon and cut into 12-mm (½-inch) pieces. In a frying pan over medium-high heat, warm the olive oil. Add the bacon pieces and fry until crisp, about 5 minutes. Using a slotted spoon, transfer the pieces to paper towels to drain, reserving the pan with the oil.

3 Away from the heat, add the pimentón and garlic to the reserved oil. Return to medium-high heat and sauté until the oil is coloured and the garlic begins to brown, about 30 seconds. Pour the garlic oil over the potato-cabbage mixture. Scatter the pork pieces over the top and serve at once.

Serve with an intensely flavoured, aromatic, silky red wine from Aragon.

CEPS AL FORN

Oven-roasted Wild Mushrooms with Garlic and Parsley

Ceps or cèpes, also known as porcini or penny bun mushrooms, are the meatiest, juiciest, and finest flavoured of all wild autumn mushrooms. They arrive in the markets of Barcelona at the beginning of October, after the first rains, and are eagerly bought. One of the best uses for this delicacy is also the simplest: oven roasted with a picada, *the mixture of herbs, ground nuts, and spices often added to Catalan dishes. The following recipe was adapted from one by writer and gastronome Pep Palau, an acknowledged expert in Catalan mushroom cookery.*

1 To clean the mushrooms, cut away the base of the stems and remove any dirt with a soft brush or a damp cloth (it is best not to wash them). Cut any large mushrooms in half or into pieces, leaving the smaller mushrooms whole.

2 In a dry frying pan over low heat, sweat the mushrooms to remove any excess moisture, about 5 minutes. Add the olive oil and season with salt and pepper. Raise the heat to medium-high and sauté, turning the mushrooms to coat all sides, for about 5 minutes. Remove from the heat and set aside.

3 Preheat the oven to 200°C (400°F). To make the *picada*, using a mortar and pestle, crush together the garlic and salt, then add the parsley and olive oil and grind until a thick, smooth paste forms, about 10 minutes. Add the breadcrumbs and mix well.

4 Butter a roasting tin in which the mushrooms will fit in a single layer. Transfer the mushrooms to the pan and drizzle the *picada* over them. Roast until the mushrooms are sizzling, about 5 minutes. Turn on the grill and grill until lightly browned, 1–2 minutes longer. Transfer to a warmed platter and serve at once.

Serve with a tannic, aromatic Spanish red wine.

450 g (1 lb) fresh ceps (porcini)

120 ml (4 fl oz) extra virgin olive oil

Salt and freshly ground pepper

FOR THE PICADA

2 cloves garlic, quartered

½ teaspoon salt

Handful of fresh flat-leaved parsley leaves, roughly chopped

1 tablespoon extra virgin olive oil

15 g (½ oz) fresh breadcrumbs

Makes 4 servings

Wild Mushrooms

The enthusiasm for wild mushrooms in Catalonia goes beyond logic and reason. Local gastronome Pep Palau chalks it up to something in the national Catalan character: a need to experience the authentic side of the culture. Whatever the explanation, the lower slopes of the Pyrenees, with their deciduous forests, are a paradise for mushroom-hunters.

Mushroom-hunting at its present level of intensity actually began no more than a decade or so ago. Llorenç Petràs, owner of the Petràs mushroom stall in La Boqueria market, and one of Catalonia's greatest authorities on fungi, remembers that twenty years ago there was only one species the Catalans would touch – the *rovelló,* or *níscalo (Lactarius deliciosus),* known in English as the saffron milk cap. They were fearful of all the rest, which they cheerfully exchanged for coffee and sugar with their French neighbours on the other side of the mountains. While *rovellons* are still a popular and sought-after species, the situation today is a very different story, and chanterelles, ceps (porcini), parasols, and at least a dozen other varieties are all very popular.

ESCALIVADA

Roasted Vegetable Salad

On summer weekends, Barcelona families like to repair to the wooded hills behind the city, where they fire up barbecues and while away the afternoon with food, wine, and naps in deck chairs. The menu on these occasions will usually feature barbecued lamb, pork, and botifarres (sausages), as well as vegetables briefly barbecued over the coals and combined to make escalivada, one of the Mediterranean's most original salads. It is another Catalan dish that is tied firmly to a particular season, in this case summer, when aubergines, sweet peppers, and tomatoes are in abundance and at their best.

4 red sweet peppers, about 1 kg (2¼ lb) total weight

2 large or 4 small aubergines, about 1 kg (2¼ lb) total weight

2 yellow onions, unpeeled

4 tomatoes, about 450 g (1 lb) total weight

1 head garlic

Coarse salt

250 ml (8 fl oz) olive oil

Extra virgin olive oil for drizzling

3 tablespoons red wine vinegar

Makes 4 servings

1 Preheat the oven to 200°C (400°F). Place the sweet peppers, aubergines, onions, tomatoes, and garlic in a single layer on a large baking sheet. Sprinkle with salt and drizzle the olive oil evenly over the top. Roast until the tomato skins have split and started to blacken, about 20 minutes. Using tongs, transfer the tomatoes to a bowl. Continue roasting the remaining vegetables, turning once, until the onions are soft and translucent and the skins of the aubergine and peppers are blistered and beginning to blacken, 25–40 minutes longer.

2 Remove the vegetables from the oven and let stand until cool enough to handle. Peel the sweet peppers, then slice each pepper in half lengthways and discard the seeds, ribs, and stems. Chop the peppers coarsely. Peel the aubergines and chop coarsely. Peel the onions and tomatoes and chop coarsely. Place the peppers, aubergines, onions, and tomatoes in a serving bowl. Separate the cloves of garlic and gently squeeze out the roasted flesh from each one. Add to the bowl with the vegetables.

3 Dress the salad with salt to taste, a drizzling of extra virgin olive oil, and the vinegar. Toss the salad gently but thoroughly and serve warm.

Serve with a fresh, fruity rosé from Navarre.

CALÇOTADA
Grilled Spring Onions with Romesco Sauce

On Saturdays and Sundays from February to April, the citizens of Barcelona jump into their cars and race down the motorways to restaurants specialising in calçotades. *Originally from Valls, this speciality has rapidly become popular throughout the region. The season's first new spring onions* (calçots) *are roasted over coals until the outer skins are blackened and the insides are sweet and tender. Diners peel off the burnt outer skins and dunk the onions in* romesco *sauce before eating them. It's a messy business requiring paper bibs.*

1 To make the sauce, prepare a fire in a charcoal-fired barbecue or preheat a gas grill on high. Grill the garlic, turning as needed, until browned on all sides, 13–15 minutes. Grill the tomatoes, turning once, until the skins are browned and wrinkled, about 5 minutes. Set aside and let cool.

2 Peel the garlic cloves. Using a large mortar and pestle, grind together the garlic and nuts. Peel the tomatoes and add to the mortar along with the French bread slices. Grind well until a thick paste forms. (Alternatively, place the peeled garlic and tomatoes, nuts, and French bread in a food processor and pulse to combine.) Mix in the olive oil, 2 tablespoons vinegar, the pimentón, and salt to taste. The finished sauce should be thick but not dry; add more oil and vinegar if needed. Divide among individual dipping bowls and set aside. (The sauce will keep in an airtight container in the refrigerator for up to 5 days; bring it to room temperature before serving.)

3 While you are making the sauce, place the onions on the barbecue or under the grill and grill, turning occasionally, until the outer skins have blackened and shrivelled, about 8 minutes. Wrap the onions in newspaper and let stand until cool enough to handle, about 5 minutes.

4 Transfer the onions to a large serving dish or a wooden board. Diners peel the onions with their fingers and dip each into the *romesco* sauce. Serve with crusty bread.

Serve with a slightly chilled, young, light-bodied Rioja.

FOR THE SAUCE

1 head garlic

2 ripe tomatoes

115 g (4 oz) blanched almonds, toasted (page 173)

60 g (2 oz) hazelnuts, toasted and skinned (page 173)

4 small slices of French bread

120 ml (4 fl oz) extra virgin olive oil, or to taste

2 tablespoons red wine vinegar, or to taste

1 teaspoon pimentón (smoked paprika) or sweet paprika

Salt

24 spring onions, each about 2.5 cm (1 inch) wide at the base and with plenty of white flesh

Crusty bread for serving

Makes 4 servings

Fiesta Foods: Calçots

Like the rest of the Iberian peninsula, Catalonia has its innumerable *festes*. But the food-related fiesta, or *aplec* – the celebration of an individual ingredient or dish – is particularly characteristic of the *països catalans*. In the last few years, such events have multiplied a hundred-fold, until it seems as if practically every town or village has its special day of tastings, feasting, and partying.

It started with the *calçotada*. *Calçots* are a type of spring onion harvested between January and February. In the Baix Camp region on the outskirts of Tarragona (of which Valls is the capital), the onions have long been roasted over coals and served with a local version of *romesco* sauce. The idea of dipping them, caramelised from the fire, into this rich sauce is inspired and delicious. At Masia Bou, a farmhouse near Valls, the hosts found themselves serving *calçots* to parties of locals. The onions were only the first course, followed by barbecued meat, but they were greeted with so much excitement that the *calçotada* was born. The custom has spread from Valls to the rest of Catalonia.

AMANIDA CATALANA
Catalan Salad

The typical Spanish ensalada mixta, with its canned asparagus, grated carrot, and sweetcorn, is a dreary dish – inexplicably so, given the enormous variety and quality of the salad ingredients grown in Spain. In Barcelona, you can easily avoid this typically unappetising combination by ordering the amanida catalana. This is one of the two national salads (the other is xató, page 109). It originated in the countryside, where it was brought to the workers at lunchtime during the summer wheat harvest. With its wealth of protein and bright colours, it must have come as a welcome sight after the heat and dust of the long morning's work.

FOR THE VINAIGRETTE

3 tablespoons red wine vinegar

Salt and freshly ground pepper

120 ml (4 fl oz) extra virgin olive oil

2 ripe tomatoes

2 hard-boiled eggs, peeled

315 g (10 oz) mixed salad greens such as romaine or cos lettuce, curly endive, and endive, torn into pieces

1 red onion, cut into thin rings

1 green sweet pepper, seeded and cut into narrow strips

6 canned anchovy fillets in olive oil

12 black olives cured in oil

4 thin slices serrano or prosciutto ham

16–20 thin slices cured sausage such as *salchichón,* salami, chorizo, or *sobrassada*

Makes 4 servings

1 To make the vinaigrette, in a bowl, whisk together the vinegar and ½ teaspoon salt. Slowly add the olive oil while whisking constantly. Taste and adjust the seasoning with salt and pepper.

2 Quarter the tomatoes and eggs lengthways and place them in a large bowl with the salad greens. Add the onion and sweet pepper and toss together along with the vinaigrette to mix evenly.

3 Pile the mixture on a large serving dish and decorate with the anchovies and olives. Cut the ham slices into 7.5 cm (3 inch) squares. Arrange the ham and sausages around the dish. Serve at once.

Serve with a jug of sangria.

CREMA DE LLENTIES

Cream of Lentil Soup with Garlic-Herb Croutons

Cal Isidre, an esteemed family-run restaurant on the Carrer Les Flors, specialises in Catalan cuisine made with luxury ingredients and enormous dedication. The lentil soup is a revelation. Puréeing the humble lentil seems to transform it completely. By nature earthy and rustic, it becomes velvety and voluptuous, like a country bumpkin magically transformed into an aristocrat. At Cal Isidre, the soup is served with a garnish of fried cansalada (cured pork fat) and botifarra negra (black pudding). In this version, the black pudding has been replaced by crisp croutons flavoured with garlic and fresh herbs.

1 To make the soup, in a saucepan over medium-high heat, combine the mineral water, lentils, single cream, butter, and ham bone. Bring to the boil, reduce the heat to medium-low, cover partially, and simmer gently until the lentils are soft but not disintegrating, about 40 minutes.

2 Discard the ham bone. In a food processor or blender, working in batches if necessary, process the lentils until smooth. Strain the purée through a fine meshed sieve. (The goal of both puréeing and straining is to reach a perfectly creamy consistency.) Return the purée to the saucepan and season to taste with salt and pepper. Cover and keep warm over low heat.

3 To make the topping, in a small, heavy frying pan over medium heat, warm the olive oil. Add the bacon and fry until crisp, about 6 minutes. Using a slotted spoon, transfer the bacon to paper towels to drain. Add the garlic to the oil in the pan and sauté until translucent, about 2 minutes. Add the bread cubes and sauté until both the garlic and bread are golden brown, about 3 minutes longer. Using a slotted spoon, transfer the croûtons and garlic to paper towels to drain. In a bowl, combine the croûtons and garlic with the bacon. Add the chopped herbs and toss gently to combine.

4 Ladle the soup into warmed individual bowls and top each serving with a quarter of the croûton mixture. Serve at once.

Serve with a light, intensely coloured young red wine such as Rioja.

FOR THE SOUP

1 l (1¾ pints) still mineral water

300 g (10½ oz) small green lentils, such as Puy lentils, rinsed

250 ml (8 fl oz) single cream

15 g (½ oz) unsalted butter

1 ham bone, about 185 g (6 oz)

Salt and freshly ground pepper

FOR THE TOPPING

60 ml (2 fl oz) extra-virgin olive oil

115 g (4 oz) lean bacon rashers, rinds removed, chopped

3 cloves garlic, thinly sliced

2 thick slices coarse country white bread, about 85 g (3 oz) total weight, crusts removed and bread cut into 2.5 cm (1 inch) cubes

Handful of mixed fresh herbs, such as chervil, flat-leaved parsley, chives, and tarragon, all finely chopped

Makes 4 servings

TRUITA AMB SUC
Spinach Omelette with Tomato Sauce

This is a variation of the traditional Spanish tortilla, *unusual because the omelette is finished in a rich tomato and garlic sauce (called* suc *in Catalan) in a terracotta dish. Once a year, the inhabitants of Ulldemolins, a town in the Priorat – one of the most beautiful wine-growing areas in the world – hold a celebration of the* truita amb suc, *with demonstrations and tastings. Each cook brings his or her own version of the dish. The omelette should contain spinach and sometimes potato, but other vegetables are often added, too. A mixture of ground nuts and parsley, or* picada, *gives an authentically Catalan finish to the dish.*

1 kg (2¼ lb) fresh spinach, stemmed, or 1 packet (440 g/ 14 oz) frozen spinach, thawed

125 ml (4 fl oz) plus 2 tablespoons olive oil

6 large eggs

Salt and freshly ground pepper

8 cloves garlic, finely chopped

1 tablespoon flour

500 ml (16 fl oz) tomato purée

1 teaspoon pimentón (smoked paprika) or sweet paprika

250 ml (8 fl oz) hot water

FOR THE PICADA

12 blanched almonds

1 tablespoon extra virgin olive oil

1 slice coarse country white bread, about 30 g (1 oz), crust removed

Handful of fresh flat-leaved parsley leaves

Crusty country bread for serving

Makes 6 servings

1 If using fresh spinach, put the spinach with just the rinsing water clinging to the leaves in a saucepan over medium-high heat. Cover and cook until the spinach is bright green and wilted, about 2 minutes. Remove from the heat and drain well in a sieve, pressing the spinach with the back of a spoon to remove excess moisture. When the spinach is cool, chop it coarsely and set aside. If using frozen spinach, drain well, pressing out all excess moisture.

2 In a wide, heavy, shallow frying pan over medium heat, warm 125 ml (4 fl oz) olive oil. Add the spinach and sauté until hot, about 2 minutes.

3 In a large bowl, beat the eggs until blended. Transfer the spinach to the bowl with the eggs and mix evenly. Season with salt and pepper. Reserve the pan with the remaining oil.

4 Return the pan containing the oil to medium heat. Gently pour the egg and spinach mixture into the pan and cook until the underside of the omelette is set and golden, about 5 minutes (use a spatula to lift the edge of the omelette to check for doneness). Remove the pan from the heat. Invert a plate on top of the pan and carefully invert the pan and plate together. Lift off the pan, letting the omelette fall onto the plate. Slide the omelette back into the pan to brown the other side, about 3 minutes longer. (If the egg mixture has stuck to the pan, brown the top under the grill instead.)

5 In a *cassola* or flameproof casserole over medium heat, warm the remaining 2 tablespoons olive oil. Add the garlic and sauté until golden, about 2 minutes.

Remove from the heat and add the flour. Return to the heat and cook, stirring constantly, until the mixture is smooth and creamy, 1–2 minutes. Add the tomato purée, pimentón, hot water, and salt to taste. Cook, stirring, until the sauce is reduced slightly but not too thick, about 5 minutes.

6 Cut the omelette into 6 pieces and slide the pieces into the *cassola* with the sauce so that the sauce almost covers them. After 15 minutes of bubbling – what the Catalans call *xup-xup* – turn off the heat.

7 To make the *picada,* in a dry frying pan over high heat, toast the almonds until golden brown, about 2 minutes. Transfer to a plate to cool. In the same pan over medium heat, warm the olive oil. Add the bread and fry on both sides until crisp, about 2 minutes on each side. Using a mortar and pestle, grind together the toasted almonds, fried bread, and parsley.

8 Transfer the omelette pieces to individual plates, top with some of the sauce, and sprinkle with the *picada*. Serve at room temperature with plenty of crusty country bread for mopping up the sauce.

Serve with a straw-coloured, herbaceous white wine from the Priorat.

CANELONS DE FESTA

Feast-Day Cannelloni

For centuries, Barcelona has maintained ties with Italy. As Colman Andrews explains in Catalan Cuisine, *the influx of Italian restaurateurs in the nineteenth century brought a number of formerly unfamiliar ingredients. Even today, many visitors are surprised at just how much pasta is consumed in Barcelona. Canelons – cannelloni stuffed with mixed meats and served with a thick béchamel – are traditionally served on feast days. In fact, if the city had a signature dish, it would probably be the rich and comforting* canelons de festa.

1 Bring a pot three-quarters full of water to the boil. Salt the water, add the pasta, and cook until al dente, 10–12 minutes. Drain and lay out on paper towels.

2 To make the béchamel sauce, in a heavy-bottomed saucepan over low heat, melt the butter. Remove the pan from the heat, sprinkle in the flour, and whisk to combine. Return to the heat and cook 2–3 minutes, stirring constantly. Add the milk little by little, whisking constantly to prevent lumps. Reduce the heat to low and cook, stirring, until the sauce coats the back of a spoon, 3–5 minutes. Season to taste with salt and pepper and add the nutmeg. Set aside and keep warm.

3 Preheat the oven to 220°C (425°F). Grease a 23 x 30 cm (9 x 12 inch) baking dish. In a frying pan over medium heat, warm the olive oil. Add the onion and garlic and sauté until softened, 3–4 minutes. Add the ham, chicken, and pork and fry until cooked through, 5–6 minutes. Add the breadcrumbs and livers and sauté 1–2 minutes. Add the wine, season with salt and pepper, stir, and cook until the wine reduces, about 4 minutes. Remove from the heat and stir in the yolks.

4 Spread 1 tablespoon filling down the middle of each pasta square. Roll into tubes and lay them, seam side downwards, side-by-side in the prepared dish.

5 Whisk three-quarters of the cheese into the sauce and pour this over the cannelloni. Sprinkle with the rest of the cheese and dot the surface with the butter. Bake until golden brown and bubbling, about 15 minutes.

Serve with a rich, berry-tasting red wine from Cigales.

Salt and freshly ground pepper

About 450 g (1 lb) dried cannelloni or lasagna squares

FOR THE BÉCHAMEL SAUCE

60 g (2 oz) unsalted butter

60 g (2 oz) plain flour

500 ml (16 fl oz) full cream milk

Pinch of freshly grated nutmeg

60 ml (2 fl oz) olive oil

1 yellow onion, finely chopped

6 cloves garlic, finely chopped

60 g (2 oz) serrano ham, shredded

225 g (8 oz) *each* lean minced chicken and pork

60 g (2 oz) fresh breadcrumbs

115 g (4 oz) chicken livers, trimmed and minced

90 ml (3 fl oz) *vi ranci,* sweet sherry, or vermouth

2 egg yolks, lightly beaten

140 g (5 oz) cured Mahón or Parmesan cheese, grated

15 g (½ oz) unsalted butter

Makes 6 servings

Italian Influences

For long periods of its history, Catalonia had more cultural contact with Italy than with the rest of Spain. As an important seaport, Barcelona maintained trade links with Italy, particularly Genoa, absorbing many Italian customs and an appreciation of the Italian aesthetic at the same time. At the end of the eighteenth century, Italian restaurateurs in Barcelona began to make foods such as spaghetti, macaroni, and saltimbocca commonplace. One of the best-loved dishes in the city uses macaroni and is called *macarrons a la catalana*. It is served *a la cassola* (in a ceramic baking dish) with a sauce of baked mincemeat, tomato, and grated Mahón cheese. These days, Italian cuisine in the form of pizza, pasta, and so on is as prominent in Barcelona as in any other world city, and Italian terms such as carpaccio, risotto, and *semifreddo* have begun to appear on the menus of the city's most creative restaurants. The pastas and ice creams produced by Sandro Desii in Espar-reguera, outside Barcelona, are a major contribution to the craze. His *fideos* and other handmade pastas are decidedly the equal of anything made in his homeland.

FARCELLETS DE COL
Pork and Cabbage Bundles

The idea of wrapping mincemeat in leaves and braising the bundles in a small amount of liquid is not unique to Catalan cooking. The Greeks and Turks are fond of using vine leaves for their dolmades. The Romanian sarmale, *ground meat wrapped in cabbage leaves, is an Easter specialty similar to* farcellets. *The success of these dishes depends on using the correct kind of cabbage: a large head with thick, loose leaves (savoy is ideal), rather than a variety with tightly packed leaves that tear easily. Served with steamed rice or crusty bread to mop up the juices,* farcellets *make a hearty autumn dish.*

16 large cabbage leaves, preferably savoy

Salt and freshly ground pepper

FOR THE SOFREGIT

90 ml (3 fl oz) olive oil

2 yellow onions, finely chopped

1 carrot, peeled and finely chopped

6 cloves garlic, finely chopped

FOR THE FILLING

285 g (10 oz) lean minced pork

285 g (10 oz) lean minced veal or beef

Salt and freshly ground pepper

1 large egg, lightly beaten

Flour for dusting

2 tablespoons olive oil or lard

120 ml (4 fl oz) dry white wine

120 ml (4 fl oz) beef, chicken, or vegetable stock or water

Makes 6–8 servings

1 Trim the tough stalk at the end of the cabbage leaves. Pour water to a depth of 2.5 cm (1 inch) into a wide, shallow pan with a tight-fitting lid. Bring to the boil over medium heat, then add a large pinch of salt. Lay the cabbage leaves in the pan, cover, and simmer just until tender, about 10 minutes. Using tongs, transfer the leaves to paper towels to drain.

2 Preheat the oven to 180°C (350°F). To make a *sofregit,* in a frying pan over medium heat, warm the olive oil. Add the onions, carrot, and garlic and sauté until the onions are softened, about 6 minutes. Spread half the *sofregit* mixture in the bottom of a *cassola* or shallow casserole.

3 To make the filling, add the pork and veal to the pan with the remaining *sofregit* mixture and cook together until the meat is lightly browned, about 8 minutes. Transfer the meat to a bowl, season well with salt and pepper, and stir in the egg.

4 Place a heaped tablespoonful of the filling in the centre of each cabbage leaf. Fold the sides of each leaf over the filling, then roll into a neat parcel roughly the size of a large egg. Seal each *farcellet* with a toothpick.

5 Dust the *farcellets* with flour. In a wide, heavy-bottomed frying pan over medium-high heat, warm the olive oil. In batches, add the *farcellets* and fry on all sides until golden brown, about 5 minutes. As you finish frying the *farcellets,* arrange them in the *cassola* on top of the *sofregit.* When all the bundles are cooked, deglaze the frying pan with the wine, scraping to stir up any browned bits. Stir in the stock and then pour the contents of the pan over the *farcellets.*

6 Cover the *cassola* and bake the *farcellets* until cooked through, about 30 minutes. Let cool for a few minutes before serving.

Serve with a full-bodied Merlot or Cabernet Sauvignon from the Alella region.

SEGONS PLATS

Steeped in tradition, hearty dishes such as *fideuà*, whole fish baked in salt, braised beef, and roasted garlic chicken are staples of the Catalan diet.

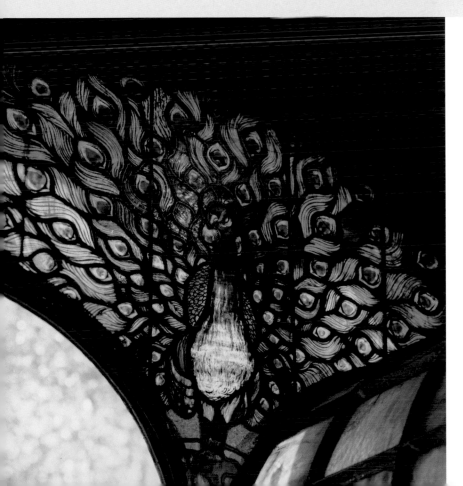

Almost every town in Catalonia contributes to the splendid variety of food in the region, from the rice dishes of the south and the fish soups and *suquets* of the north to the game stews of the Pyrenees and the barbecued meat dishes popular all over the country. Vegetables are an integral part of the Barcelona menu and are incorporated into most classic main courses. With rustic dishes like *pollastre rostit* (roasted chicken) and *civet de senglar* (wild boar stew), an entrée or side-dish can be dispensed with if you are generous with the appetisers. A simple green salad served with the *segon plat* may be all these dishes need for accompaniment.

PAELLA PARELLADA

Shellfish and Mixed Meat Paella

The name Parellada crops up regularly in Catalan food lore, partly thanks to Ramón and Ada Parellada, two pillars of the Barcelona restaurant scene, and partly due to their father, Paco, who owned the venerable Set Portes restaurant, originally founded in 1836 and still one of the city's most popular eating places. In the 1940s, Senyor Parellada began serving the Parellada paella *at Set Portes. The dish has since become the restaurant's house speciality and a classic of Barcelona eating. Though originally from Valencia, paella has spread all around the Spanish Mediterranean, with every region boasting its own version.*

1 In a saucepan over medium heat, bring the stock to a gentle simmer and maintain over low heat.

2 To prepare the artichokes, fill a bowl with water and stir in the lemon juice. Working with 1 artichoke at a time, remove the tough outer leaves. Slice off the top 5 cm (2 inches) of the remaining leaves. Cut the stem off flush with the base and discard it. Cut each artichoke lengthways into quarters, then scrape out and discard the fuzzy choke with a spoon or small, sharp knife. Place the cleaned artichoke quarters in the lemon water. Repeat with the remaining artichokes.

3 Using a mortar and pestle, grind 1 teaspoon salt with the saffron into a powder. Add the garlic and grind with the salt and saffron. Set aside. Cut the chicken thigh meat, pork loin, and sausages into 2.5 cm (1 inch) pieces. Slice the squid into rings, leaving the tentacles whole.

4 Place a 40 cm (16 inch) paella pan or a large, wide heavy-bottomed frying pan over high heat (or over a metal ring set on a rack over coals) and add the olive oil. When the oil is hot, add the chicken, pork, squid, and sausages and fry until golden, about 10 minutes. Use a slotted spoon to transfer the meat and seafood to a plate and set aside. Reserve pan containing the oil.

5 Drain the artichokes and add to the paella pan. Add the onion and pepper and fry over medium heat until the onion is translucent and beginning to brown, about 3 minutes. Return the meat and squid to the pan and add the tomatoes, stirring so that the tomatoes are evenly distributed. Add 2 ladlefuls of the hot stock and allow to simmer for 1–2 minutes.

6 Stir a little stock into the mortar with the saffron mixture and mix well. Pour the contents of the mortar into the saucepan of stock.

7 Add the rice to the meat and vegetables in the paella pan, followed by the peas and all but 120 ml (4 fl oz) of the remaining stock. Stir everything together thoroughly.

8 Cut the monkfish into 2.5 cm (1 inch) pieces. Scrub the mussels with a stiff brush. Remove the beards by scraping the tuft of fibres off with a knife. Remove them from their shells if desired. Arrange the fish, mussels, and prawns on top of the rice mixture, discarding any mussels that do not close to the touch. Return the paella to a simmer and cook until the meat and fish are cooked through and the rice is tender but not too soft, about 20 minutes. If mussels are in their shells, discard any that have failed to open. If the paella is not yet done and all the liquid is absorbed, add a little of the reserved stock as needed.

9 Turn off the heat and cover the pan with a clean, dry kitchen towel. Let stand for about 10 minutes to allow the flavours to mingle thoroughly and the rice to absorb any remaining juices. Serve warm, not hot, garnished with the parsley.

Serve with a juicy, fresh young white wine such as Rueda or Verdejo.

---

1 l (1¾ pints) chicken stock

Juice of ½ lemon

4 large globe artichokes

Coarse sea salt

1 teaspoon saffron threads

3 cloves garlic, thinly sliced

6 chicken thighs, boned

150 g (5½ oz) pork loin

225 g (8 oz) pork sausages

200 g (7 oz) cleaned squid

250 ml (8 fl oz) olive oil

1 yellow onion, thinly sliced

1 red sweet pepper, seeded and cut into 2.5 cm (1 inch) pieces

450 g (1 lb) ripe tomatoes, peeled, seeded (page 187), and finely chopped

450 g (1 lb) short-grain (Italian) rice

150 g (5½ oz) shelled garden peas, fresh or frozen

175 g (6 oz) monkfish or hake fillet

24 large mussels

12 medium-size prawns, peeled

Fresh flat-leaved parsley

Makes 8 servings

FRICANDÓ AMB MOIXERNONS

Braised Beef with Mushrooms

The mushrooms most commonly used for fricandó, *a rich, dark, delicious beef stew, are* moixernons, Marasmius oreades, *the fairy ring champignon, which grows all over the temperate zones of Europe and North America. They are sold at Llorenç Petràs's mushroom stall at Barcelona's La Boqueria market (page 25), and elsewhere in Catalonia, and can be bought dried from mail-order and online sources (page 187). Left to soak overnight, they will perfume your kitchen with a fragrance of autumn woods and damp earth. If they are unavailable, substitute other mushrooms.* Fricandó *is traditionally served with sautéed potatoes.*

140 g (5 oz) flour

Salt and freshly ground pepper

1 kg (2¼ lb) beef rump, chuck, or topside, cut into slices 12 mm (½ inch) thick

80 ml (3 fl oz) olive oil

2 *each* fresh oregano, thyme, and marjoram sprigs or 1 teaspoon *each* dried oregano, thyme, and marjoram

1 fresh rosemary sprig or ½ teaspoon dried rosemary

2 yellow onions, thinly sliced

2 tomatoes, cored

3 cloves garlic, crushed

250 ml (8 fl oz) dry white wine

1 bay leaf

2 pinches of freshly grated nutmeg

30 g (1 oz) bitter chocolate

60 g (2 oz) dried wild mushrooms, soaked in water to cover overnight

750 ml (24 fl oz) beef stock

Makes 6 servings

1 Place the flour in a shallow bowl, season with salt and pepper, and stir to combine. Lightly dredge the beef slices on both sides in the seasoned flour, shaking off any excess.

2 In a heavy-bottomed casserole over medium heat, warm the olive oil. Working in batches if necessary, add the beef and brown on all sides, about 5 minutes. Transfer the beef to a plate with a slotted spoon. Reserve the pot with the remaining oil.

3 Next, make a *sofregit*. If using fresh oregano, thyme, marjoram, and rosemary sprigs, tie them in a bundle with kitchen string and set aside. Return the pot to medium heat, add the onions, and fry until soft, about 3 minutes. Cut the tomatoes in half and, using the large holes of a grater, grate the pulp directly into the pot. Discard the skins. Add the garlic. When the vegetables are cooked, after about 4 minutes, add the wine. Add the herb bundle or dried herbs and the bay leaf and nutmeg. Then grate the chocolate directly into the pot. Simmer over medium heat until the ingredients begin to form a sauce, about 5 minutes.

4 Drain the mushrooms in a sieve lined with muslin, reserving the liquid, and add to the pot. Return the beef to the pot with any juices. Add the stock and enough of the mushroom-soaking liquid to cover the beef. Season to taste with salt and pepper.

5 Reduce the heat to low, cover partially, and cook until the beef is thoroughly tender and the sauce is thick and concentrated, about 1 hour. If using fresh herbs, remove and discard the herb bundle, then discard the bay leaf. Transfer to a warmed serving dish or serve straight from the casserole.

Serve with a rich, beefy tannic red wine from the Montsant or Priorat.

BACALLÀ AMB SAMFAINA

Salt Cod with Aubergine, Sweet Peppers, Onion, and Tomato

Salt cod is one of the staple foods of Catalonia and serving it in samfaina *is one of the most popular ways of preparing it. Samfaina is reminiscent of French ratatouille, a simple stew of Mediterranean summer vegetables such as aubergines, sweet peppers, onions and tomatoes, although in Catalonia it is considered a sauce rather than something to be eaten on its own. The slight sweetness of the vegetables balances the saltiness of the cod.* Bacallà amb samfaina *needs no accompaniment other than a basket of good crusty bread.*

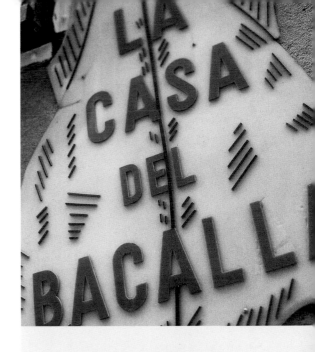

1 To prepare the salt cod, place it in a large bowl of cold water, cover and refrigerate for 3 days, changing the water once a day.

2 To make the *samfaina,* sprinkle the aubergines with salt and drain them in a colander set over a bowl for about 1 hour. Rinse and thoroughly dry. Meanwhile, place the tomatoes in a food processor or blender and purée them. Set the purée aside.

3 In a large frying pan over medium heat, warm the olive oil. Add the aubergines, onion and sweet peppers and cook gently until the vegetables are soft, about 5 minutes. Stir in the tomato purée and season with a generous grinding of pepper. (Do not add salt, as the cod will season the dish while cooking.) Cook, stirring occasionally, until thickened, about 20 minutes. Remove from the heat, cover and set aside.

4 Drain the salt cod, remove any bones or skin and cut into 7.5-cm (3-inch) chunks. Dust with flour. In a wide, shallow saucepan over medium-high heat, warm the 2 tablespoons olive oil. Add the cod and fry gently, moving the pieces as little as possible to keep them whole, until lightly browned, 5 minutes.

5 Transfer the cod pieces to the frying pan so that each piece is surrounded by sauce. Place over low heat, cover and cook until the sauce is bubbling around the fish, about 10 minutes. Sprinkle with the parsley and let cool slightly before serving.

Serve with a rich, well-balanced Spanish red wine.

750 g (1½ lb) salt cod

FOR THE SAMFAINA

1 large or 2 small aubergines, cut into 12-mm (½-inch) dice

Salt and freshly ground pepper

3 or 4 large, ripe tomatoes, about 450 g (1 lb) total weight, peeled and seeded (page 187)

125 ml (4 fl oz) olive oil

1 large yellow onion, cut into ½-inch (12-mm) dice

1 red sweet pepper, seeded and cut into 12-mm (½-inch) dice

1 green sweet pepper, seeded and cut into 12-mm (½-inch) dice

Flour for dusting

2 tablespoons olive oil

Leaves from 6 fresh flat-leaved parsley sprigs, finely chopped

Makes 4–6 servings

La Casa del Bacallà

Salt cod is old-fashioned, frugal food. In central Spain, in the days before refrigerators, it served to satisfy the demand for fish, as the salting process enabled it to be stored almost indefinitely. *Bacallà a la llauna,* salt cod baked in olive oil in a rectangular baking tin called a *llauna,* is often cited as the signature dish of Barcelona, although it is not often seen on restaurant menus nowadays. *Bacallà amb samfaina,* with the typical Catalan sauce of aubergines, sweet peppers, onion and tomato, is still a popular dish all over the region. Salt cod appears in many other dishes as well, from *esqueixada* (shredded in a salad) to *bunyols* (savoury fritters) to *coques.*

La Casa del Bacallà is part of a nationwide chain that sells only cod from the Faroe Islands, regarded as the finest. Various cuts are available, from *morro* or *lomo* (the fattest and leanest, good for roasting) to *ventresca* (belly), *kokotxa* (cheeks), and *desmigado* (broken into small chunks). The fish must be desalted before use, typically by soaking it in plenty of cold water that is changed daily over three or four days.

CALDERETA DE LLAGOSTA
Lobster Soup

The little port of Fornells, on Minorca's rocky north coast, has set itself up as the capital of caldereta. *King Juan Carlos has even been known to drop in at Es Plà, the most famous restaurant in town, when sailing past on his yacht. The* caldereta *is a classic Mediterranean lobster dish, featuring sweet peppers, tomatoes, garlic, and parsley. Spiny lobsters (langoustines), a species without big claws, are the traditional crustaceans used in this dish, but "true" lobsters will also do here. They must be live, however, as lobster meat deteriorates rapidly. When purchasing, look for a lively lobster that is heavy for its size and has a hard shell.*

4 small live lobsters, about 450 g (1 lb) each

1 bay leaf

6 peppercorns

80 ml (3 fl oz) olive oil

1 yellow onion, finely chopped

1 red or green sweet pepper, seeded and chopped

1 large ripe tomato, peeled, seeded (page 187), and chopped

1 celery stalk, chopped

3 cloves garlic, finely chopped

¼ cup fresh flat-leaved parsley sprigs, finely chopped

Salt

4 slices coarse country bread, about 115 g (4 oz) total weight, toasted

Makes 4 servings

1 Bring a large pot three-quarters full of water to the boil over high heat. Immerse the live lobsters in the water and leave for 2 minutes, just long enough to kill them. Lift out with tongs and set on a work surface. When cool enough to handle, using a small, sharp knife, make a lengthways cut along the underside of each lobster. Remove and discard the small intestine in the centre of the tail. Detach and reserve the heads and legs, then cut each lobster horizontally into 4–6 pieces. Using a lobster cracker or mallet, gently crack the claws, if using "true" lobsters.

2 Remove the sand sac from the lobster head. If desired, scoop the creamy coral out of the heads, scramble with a fork in a small bowl, and set aside.

3 Use the reserved heads and legs to make the lobster stock: Place them in a saucepan with 40 fl oz (2 pints) water, the bay leaf, and the peppercorns and bring to the boil over high heat. Reduce the heat to medium and simmer about 15 minutes.

4 In a *cassola* or casserole over medium heat, warm the olive oil. Add the onion, sweet pepper, tomato, celery, garlic, and parsley and fry until the onion is softened, about 5 minutes. Stir in the reserved lobster coral, then add the lobster pieces, turning them so that they are well coated.

5 Strain the lobster stock through a colander or sieve lined with muslin, discarding the heads and legs, bay leaf, and peppercorns. Add 1 l (1¾ pints) of the stock to the *cassola* and bring to a boil over high heat. Reduce the heat to medium and cook until the flesh turns opaque, about 10 minutes. Season to taste with salt.

6 To serve, place a slice of toast in each shallow soup bowl and divide the lobster pieces evenly among them. Ladle the stock and vegetables over the top and serve at once.

Serve with a rich, full-bodied, oak-aged Spanish Chardonnay from the Penedès.

ARRÒS AMB CROSTA

Baked Rice with Chicken, Sausage, and Chick-peas

The town of Elche, in the southern part of the Catalan-speaking region, is famous for three very disparate things: the Dama de Elche, an ancient sculpture of a female figure; the Misteri de Elx, a religious drama enacted once a year in the local church; and the spectacular grove of palm trees that dates back to the presence of the Moors during the Middle Ages. Elche has a fourth claim to fame: this signature dish, a kind of paella of mixed meats and rice with a thin crust of beaten egg. It is delicious and lovely to look at, emerging from the oven with a golden yellow crust puffed up slightly around the meat, bean, and rice filling.

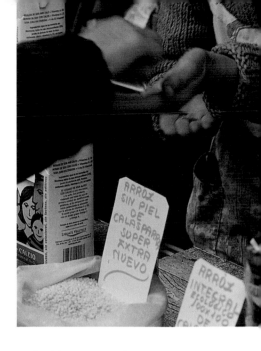

1 To make the stock, tie the herb sprigs and bay leaf in a square of muslin using kitchen string and place in a large, heavy-bottomed stockpot with 1 l (1¾ pints) water, the turnip, carrot, and onion. Bring to the boil over high heat. Reduce the heat to medium and simmer, uncovered, for 20 minutes.

2 In a bowl, mix the pork with the fresh breadcrumbs and season well with salt and pepper. Form into balls about the size of small walnuts and roll the meatballs in the dried breadcrumbs. Set aside.

3 Cut each chicken thigh into 2 pieces. Season the rabbit and chicken pieces with salt and pepper. In a *cassola* or casserole over medium heat, warm the ½ cup olive oil. Add the rabbit and chicken and fry, turning as needed, until browned on all sides, about 6 minutes. Using a slotted spoon, transfer to the stockpot, reserving the remaining oil in the *cassola*.

4 Cut the pork sausages into 5-cm (2-inch) pieces. Return the *cassola* to medium heat and fry the sausage pieces until nicely browned, about 4 minutes. Using the slotted spoon, transfer to paper towels to drain, reserving the remaining oil in the *cassola*.

5 In a separate frying pan over medium heat, warm the 2 tablespoons oil. Add the meatballs and fry, turning, until golden brown, about 5 minutes. Using the slotted spoon, transfer to paper towels to drain.

6 Using a mortar and pestle, grind 1 teaspoon salt with the saffron threads until a deep yellow powder forms. Add the parsley and grind together to form a thick paste. Set aside.

7 Preheat the oven to 220°C (425°F). Return the *cassola* and oil to medium-high heat, add the garlic, and fry until soft, about 2 minutes. (This may seem like a lot of garlic, but it is only used to flavour the oil.) Using the slotted spoon, remove the garlic from the pan and discard it. Add the rice and fry in the hot oil for about 30 seconds, then add the tomato and stir together for 30 seconds longer. Add 750 ml (1¼ pints) of the stock, the rabbit and chicken pieces and the sausage, then stir in the saffron-parsley mixture. Cook without stirring until all the liquid is absorbed, 12–15 minutes. Test the rice; the grains should be tender but not entirely soft. If further cooking is necessary, add a little more stock as needed. Remove from the heat and scatter the chick-peas and meatballs over the rice.

8 In a small bowl, beat the eggs with a whisk and pour them evenly over the rice. Immediately transfer to the oven and bake until the egg crust is opaque and beginning to brown, about 10 minutes. Remove from the oven and let cool slightly before serving.

Serve with a robust, full-bodied red wine from the Alicante.

6 mixed fresh herb sprigs such as thyme, oregano, and rosemary

1 bay leaf

1 *each* turnip, carrot, and small yellow onion, peeled and chopped

185 g (6 oz) minced pork

60 g (2 oz) fresh breadcrumbs

Sea salt and freshly ground pepper

60 g (2 oz) dry breadcrumbs

2 *each* chicken thighs and rabbit or chicken legs

120 ml (4 fl oz) olive oil, plus 2 tablespoons

155 g (5½ oz) pork sausages

1 teaspoon saffron threads

Leaves from 3 fresh flat-leaved parsley sprigs

6 cloves garlic, coarsely chopped

255 g (9 oz) short-grain rice such as Bomba

1 large tomato, peeled and chopped

150 g (5½ oz) drained, canned chick-peas

4 large eggs

Makes 4 servings

POLLASTRE ROSTIT
Roast Chicken with Garlic

Catalan cooks have always known the value of a fine roasting chicken. The region even has its own Denominació d'Origen *for chickens, called* Pollastre del Prat. *The most popular method of cooking chicken is either in a* samfaina *(page 141) or barbecued over a charcoal fire, closely followed by roasting in a terra-cotta* cassola. *The classic Mediterranean combination of garlic, tomatoes, herbs, and wine fills the kitchen with glorious aromas as the chicken browns and sizzles. Although the preparation is essentially simple, it is truly a dish for special occasions – what the Catalans call* un plat de festa.

1 roasting chicken, preferably free-range, about 1.35 kg (3 lb), cut into 8 serving pieces

Salt and freshly ground pepper

60 g (2 oz) lard (optional)

60 ml (2 fl oz) olive oil

8 cloves garlic, peeled

250 ml (8 fl oz) *vi ranci,* sweet sherry, or vermouth

2 yellow onions, cut into thick chunks

2 fresh oregano sprigs

2 bay leaves

4 small, ripe tomatoes, about 175 g (6 oz) total weight

Makes 4 servings

1 Preheat the oven to 350°F (180°C). Generously season the chicken pieces all over with salt and pepper. In a heavy frying pan over medium heat, melt the lard, if using, with the olive oil. Add the chicken pieces and cook, turning as needed, until golden brown on all sides, about 6 minutes. Add the garlic and cook for about 1 minute longer, then pour in the wine. Remove from the heat.

2 Distribute the onions in the bottom of a *cassola,* an ovenproof ceramic baking dish, or a round baking dish about 25 cm (10 inches) in diameter. Arrange the chicken pieces on top of the onions. Shred the oregano and bay leaves over the chicken. Prick the

tomatoes once or twice with the point of a sharp knife and place them among the chicken pieces. (The tomato juices will seep out as they cook, contributing to the sauce that forms at the bottom of the *cassola.*) Pour the pan juices and the garlic over the meat.

3 Roast, turning the chicken pieces once or twice so that they brown evenly, until the meat is evenly browned and the skin is crisp, 45–60 minutes. Serve warm from the *cassola* or transfer to a serving dish.

Serve with a dry sparkling white wine such as *cava* from Juvé i Camps, Codorníu, or Agustí Torelló.

POLLASTRE AMB GAMBES

Braised Chicken with Prawns

Barcelona food is full of surprises. Visitors may find the combinations of fish and meat strange, with such mixtures as snails and pig's trotters bordering on the surreal. But such dishes are not unusual even on the daily menu at unassuming places such as Barcelona's El Celler Vell, an informal eatery where this classic prawn and chicken dish is offered. In its hometown of Tossa de Mar, a fishing village turned resort on the Costa Brava, the prawns are sometimes replaced by lobster. In either case, it is a luxurious pairing.

1 Place the flour in a shallow bowl, season with salt and pepper, and stir to combine. Toss the chicken pieces in the flour, shaking off any excess.

2 In a large frying pan over medium heat, warm 2 tablespoons of the olive oil. Add the chicken pieces and cook, turning as needed, until golden brown on all sides, about 10 minutes. Using a slotted spoon, transfer the chicken to a casserole or baking dish with a tight-fitting lid.

3 Add the *vi ranci* to the pan. Deglaze over medium heat, stirring to scrape up any browned bits. Let cook until the liquid is reduced by about one-third, about 5 minutes. Add the tomato passata, onion, garlic, parsley, and pimentón. Cook for about 30 seconds, then pour the liquid over the chicken pieces and stir to coat them in the sauce. Add 125 ml (4 fl oz) water, cover, and cook over low heat, stirring occasionally, until the chicken is tender, about 40 minutes.

4 Meanwhile, in a frying pan over medium heat, warm the remaining 1 tablespoon olive oil. Add the prawns and fry just until opaque, about 2 minutes. When the chicken has been cooking for 35 minutes, add the cooked prawns and pine nuts.

5 Using a mortar and pestle, grind together the liver and almonds. Add the liver mixture to the chicken and prawns and mix thoroughly. Cook for 5 minutes longer to allow the flavours to mingle, then remove from the heat. Let cool slightly before serving.

Serve with a juicy Spanish rosé with hints of raspberry.

---

150 g (5½ oz) flour

Salt and freshly ground pepper

1 chicken, 1–1.1 kg (2¼–2½ lb), cut into 10 cm (4 inch) pieces (about 12 pieces)

3 tablespoons olive oil

120 ml (4 fl oz) *vi ranci*, sweet sherry, or vermouth

250 ml (8 fl oz) tomato passata or juice

½ yellow onion, finely chopped

2 or 3 cloves garlic, finely chopped

2 tablespoons finely chopped fresh flat-leaved parsley

1 teaspoon pimentón (smoked paprika) or sweet paprika

16 medium-size raw prawns in the shell, about 450 g (1 lb) total weight

1 tablespoon pine nuts

1 chicken liver, trimmed

60 g (2 oz) blanched almonds

Makes 4 servings

Mar i Muntanya

If there is one Catalan speciality that is liable to surprise even sophisticated diners, it is *mar i muntanya*, literally 'sea and mountain'. The classic paella, with its combination of shellfish and chicken, is a more familiar *mar i muntanya* dish. But in the Empordà and along the Costa Brava, as well as in Majorca and Valencia, the fondness for mixing meat and seafood has given rise to some extraordinary dishes.

Perhaps the most accessible and best-known example of this tradition is *pollastre amb gambes*. But there are few limits to variations on this theme. Cuttlefish are cooked with sausages, squid are stuffed with meat, and suckling pig is baked with grouper. You can even enjoy a terrine of pigs' trotters with snails at a restaurant near Figueres. Food critic Jaume Fàbrega tells of a dish from the marshlands near Valencia that features eel, chicken, and beans. At the furthest extreme, there is a dish from Empordà called simply *mar i muntanya*, whose ingredients include prawns, mussels, langoustines, sausages, pigs' trotters, rabbit, chicken, snails, and wild mushrooms.

LLOM AMB PRESSECS

Pork Loin with Peaches

Jordi Alsina, arguably Barcelona's finest charcutier, has his shop and headquarters in the Sants district. It seems an unprepossessing place, until you realise the amazing variety of homemade sausages, hams, bacon, and all manner of pork products that cram the tiny space. Jordi, whose family has owned and operated the business since 1883, seems to know more than anyone about the range of Catalan sausages, and he makes most of them in the butchery behind the shop. This simple dish of roasted pork loin with fresh peaches is similar to one made by Alsina.

150 g (5½ oz) flour

Salt and freshly ground pepper

4 boneless pork loin chops, about 450 g (1 lb) total weight and each about 2 cm (¾ inch) thick

90 ml (3 fl oz) olive oil, or as needed

120 ml (4 fl oz) cognac

1 yellow onion, chopped

2 tomatoes, peeled, seeded (page 187), and chopped

500 ml (16 fl oz) chicken stock, or as needed

180 ml (6 fl oz) peach juice

3 whole, ripe peaches, about 450 g (1 lb) total weight

Makes 4 servings

1 Place the flour in a shallow bowl, season with salt and pepper, and stir to combine. Lightly dredge the pork slices on both sides in the seasoned flour, shaking off any excess.

2 In a heavy-bottomed frying pan over medium heat, warm the olive oil. Add the pork and fry, turning once, until golden brown, about 3 minutes on each side. Using a slotted spoon, transfer the pork to a warmed *cassola* or ceramic baking dish and set aside, away from the heat. Reserve the pan containing the oil.

3 In a small saucepan over low heat, warm the cognac, about 15 seconds. Pour over the pork. Averting your face, use a long kitchen match to ignite the cognac. When the alcohol has burned off, the flames will die out. (Keep a pan lid ready in case the flames flare up.)

4 In the reserved frying pan, make a *sofregit:* Warm the oil remaining in the pan over medium heat, adding a little more olive oil if needed. Add the onion and fry until softened, about 3 minutes. Add the tomatoes and cook until they have darkened in colour, 2–3 minutes. Add the stock and the peach juice and season to taste with salt and pepper. Raise the heat to high and bring to the boil, then reduce the

heat to medium-low and simmer until the sauce begins to thicken, 2–3 minutes. Pour this over the pork loin chops in the *cassola.* Cook over medium heat until the pork is tender, about 30 minutes.

5 Meanwhile, peel the peaches. Bring a saucepan three-quarters full of water to the boil. Cut an X in the blossom end of each peach. Immerse in the boiling water until the skin begins to curl away from the X, about 30 seconds. Using a slotted spoon, transfer to a bowl of ice water to cool, then peel away the skin. Cut each peach in half lengthways, remove the stone, and slice into segments.

6 Add the peaches to the *cassola,* spooning a little of the sauce over them. Cook, adding a little more stock if necessary, until the peaches are soft but not falling apart, about 7 minutes longer.

7 Arrange the pork slices neatly on a shallow serving dish and place the peaches around them. Spoon the sauce over the top and serve.

Serve with a fruity, young red wine from the Penedès.

ESCUDELLA I CARN D'OLLA

Two-Course Mixed Stew of Beans, Meat, and Vegetables

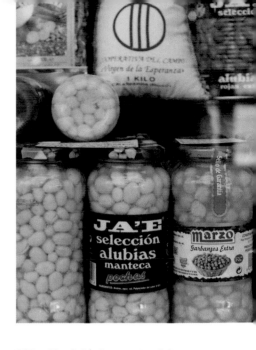

In its prime, perhaps thirty years ago, escudella *was one of the most familiar of all Catalan dishes. It is reported to have been served in some households five or six times a week, with the result that many people became heartily fed up with it, so nowadays the dish is much less common than it deserves to be. Similar to a French pot-au-feu, the* escudella *is basically a slow-cooked stew of mixed meat, vegetables, and beans that is divided into two courses: the broth, to which rice or pasta is usually added, and the* carn d'olla *(literally, "meat of the pot"), which is served with a vinaigrette dressing.*

1 Soak the dried *mongetes del ganxet* or chick-peas overnight in water to cover.

2 Fill a large stockpot two-thirds full of water and add the beef, lamb, *panceta,* chicken, and ham bone. Bring to the boil over high heat, uncovered, skimming off any foam that rises to the surface. Reduce the heat to low and simmer for 1 hour, skimming regularly.

3 Drain the beans, then add to the stockpot and simmer for 1 hour longer.

4 Peel and chop the carrots, parsnips, and turnips. Chop the celery and the white and pale green parts of the leeks. Cut the potatoes into 3 inch (7.5 cm) pieces. Add the carrots, parsnips, turnips, celery, leeks, potatoes, onion, and cabbage to the stockpot and simmer for 1 hour.

5 Meanwhile, make the meatballs: In a bowl, mix together the pork, veal, finely chopped garlic, egg, and half the parsley and season with salt and pepper. Form the mixture into 10 small balls and dust generously with the flour. Keep in the refrigerator until ready to use.

6 After the stew has simmered a total of 3 hours, the beans should be thoroughly tender, the vegetables softened, and the liquid reduced by half. Taste the broth; it should have enough flavour to stand on its own as a soup. Season generously with salt and pepper.

7 Reduce the heat to low and place the sausages and meatballs on top of the other ingredients. Cover the pot and cook until the sausages and meatballs are firm and opaque, about 30 minutes.

8 Meanwhile, mince the remaining parsley leaves. In a small bowl, combine the vinegar, crushed garlic, and finely chopped parsley. Add the olive oil in a thin stream, whisking constantly. Season to taste with salt and pepper. Set the *vinagreta* aside.

9 Remove the pot from the heat and ladle out as much of the broth as possible, pouring it through a sieve into a saucepan. In a small frying pan over medium heat, toast the saffron, about 5 seconds. Transfer the saffron to a mortar and pestle and grind to a powder. Add the saffron and *fideos* to the broth and simmer over low heat until the noodles are soft, about 4 minutes. Ladle into soup bowls for the first course.

10 To serve the second course, slice the sausages and arrange the meat and vegetables on a separate serving platter. Drizzle with some of the *vinagreta* and serve the remaining *vinagreta* on the side.

Serve with a concentrated, powerful Spanish red wine from the Priorat.

---

200 g (7 oz) dried *mongetes del ganxet* or chick-peas

450-g (1-lb) piece *each* beef rib, stewing lamb, and *panceta*

½ chicken, about 450 g (1 lb)

185-g (6-oz) piece ham bone

2 *each* carrots, parsnips, turnips, celery stalks, and leeks

4 russet potatoes, peeled

1 large yellow onion, chopped

¼ head green cabbage, sliced

175 g (6 oz) *each* minced pork and veal

3 cloves garlic, 2 finely chopped, 1 crushed

1 large egg

Leaves of 8 sprigs fresh flat-leaved parsley

Salt and freshly ground pepper

Flour for dusting

2 blood puddings (optional)

225 g (½ lb) raw pork sausages

2 tablespoons red wine vinegar

120 ml (4 fl oz) olive oil

Generous pinch of saffron threads

150 g (5½ oz) *fideos* or vermicelli

Makes 10–12 servings

ÀNEC AMB PANSES I CASTANYES

Roast Duck with Raisins and Chestnuts

While barely seen in other parts of Spain, duck is much eaten in Barcelona, where the dish is practically omnipresent along the French border with Catalonia. Traditional preparations of duck include braising with turnips or roasting with apples. This is not one of those classic dishes, but it is so authentically Catalan in spirit that it might as well be. This recipe is inspired by one from Josep Lladonosa i Giró, one of Catalonia's most famous gastronomes. His book, La Cuina Que Torna, *published in 1979, revolutionised the Catalan food scene with recipes for dishes that were then either extinct or rarely seen.*

125 g (4½ oz) raisins

225 g (½ lb) fresh chestnuts, blanched and peeled (page 185), or vacuum-packed chestnuts

Salt and freshly ground pepper

1 duck, about 1.35 kg (3 lb)

Generous pinch of freshly grated nutmeg

2 small yellow onions, coarsely chopped

1 tablespoon plain flour

250 ml (8 fl oz) dry white wine

250 ml (8 fl oz) *moscatel* or other sweet wine

60 g (2 oz) pine nuts

Makes 4 servings

1 In a bowl, soak the raisins in cold water to cover until they have plumped up slightly, about 1 hour. Drain and set aside.

2 If using fresh chestnuts, bring a large saucepan three-quarters full of water to the boil. Salt the water, add the chestnuts, and cook until tender but still whole and not mushy, about 10 minutes. Drain and set aside.

3 Preheat the oven to 180°C (350°F). Remove any giblets from the cavity of the duck and reserve for another use or discard. Rinse the duck inside and out and pat dry. Holding the blade of a sharp knife almost parallel to the skin, push the tip through the skin to make small slits all over the breast and thighs. Do not penetrate the flesh. This will help release some of the fat when the duck is roasting. Season well, inside and out, with salt and pepper and the nutmeg. Place in a roasting pan breast side up and roast until the duck is beginning to brown on top, about 45 minutes.

4 Surround the duck with the onions and roast for 15 minutes longer. Add the chestnuts, sprinkle them evenly with the flour, and stir to combine with the onions. Pour the white wine and *moscatel* over the duck

and roast for 15 minutes longer.

5 Using a wooden spoon or spatula to lift the bird, tip any cooking juices from the cavity into the onion-and-chestnut mixture and then transfer the duck to a serving dish. Add the raisins and pine nuts to the pan, season to taste with salt and pepper, and stir well, distributing the mixture evenly over the bottom of the pan. Return the duck to the pan and roast until the skin is golden brown and crisp, 10–20 minutes longer.

6 Transfer the duck to a serving dish and, using a slotted spoon, arrange the chestnuts, raisins, pine nuts and onions around the duck. Alternatively, transfer the duck to a carving board and cut into serving pieces with a large, sharp knife or heavy-duty kitchen scissors. Arrange on a serving dish, skin side up, with the chestnuts, raisins, pine nuts, and onions.

7 To serve, skim off as much fat as possible from the pan juices, then drizzle over the duck and pass the rest at the table.

Serve with a complex, powerful red wine such as an oak-aged red from the Priorat.

CIVET DE PORC

Pork Stew with Picada

In 1975, Josep Maria Boix opened a restaurant in the mountains of the Cerdanya. Almost thirty years later, it has become one of the best-loved restaurants in Catalonia – so much so that Josep Maria opened a branch in Barcelona, called Boix de Cerdanya. The restaurant serves as an urban showcase for the earthy and powerful cuisine of the Pyrenees – of which civet de senglar, a delicious dish of wild boar simmered in red wine, is one of the high points. This is a version of that traditional recipe that works well for pork. The picada, a rich, nutty paste featuring bitter chocolate, is reminiscent of Mexican mole.

1 Cut the pork into 5 cm (2 inch) cubes. In a large glass or non-reactive bowl, combine the pork, onion, carrots, leek, tomatoes, garlic, lemon, peppercorns, thyme, and bay leaves. Add the wine, cover, and marinate in the refrigerator, stirring once, for at least 24 hours or up to 2 days.

2 Transfer the pork cubes to a colander to drain. Reserve the remaining marinade ingredients in the bowl. Dry the pork with a clean kitchen towel.

3 In a Dutch oven or other heavy-bottomed pot with a lid over medium heat, melt the butter with the olive oil. Working in batches, add the pork and cook, turning as needed, until lightly browned on all sides, about 8 minutes. Using a slotted spoon, transfer the pork to a plate. Strain the reserved marinade. Set aside the liquid and discard the lemon half. Raise the heat under the pot to medium-high, add the vegetables and herbs from the marinade, and fry them in the same oil used for the pork until the onion is softened and almost all the liquid has evaporated, about 5 minutes. Remove from the heat.

4 Bring the strained marinade liquid to the boil in a small saucepan over high heat and cook until reduced by half, about 15 minutes.

5 Return the pork to the pot, reserving the vegetables. Add the reduced marinade and enough of the stock to cover the meat (you may not need all of it;

be sure to reserve at least 125 ml/4 fl oz). Place over low heat and simmer, uncovered, until the pork is fork-tender, about 1 hour.

6 Remove from the heat and, using the slotted spoon, transfer the pork to a bowl. Discard the bay leaves, thyme sprig, and peppercorns. Push the rest of the sauce through a fine-meshed sieve. Alternatively, process briefly in a food processor. Return both the sauce and pork to the pot, season with salt, stir well, cover, and continue to simmer gently over low heat, adding a little more stock if the mixture seems dry, until the sauce is thick, 10–15 minutes.

7 To make the *picada*, cut off the crust from the bread slice. In a small frying pan over medium high heat, fry the bread in the olive oil until crisp, about 2 minutes. Remove from the heat. Using a mortar and pestle, grind together the bread, nuts, chocolate, and parsley until a dark, crumbly paste forms. Stir the *picada* into the sauce and let it simmer gently for 5–10 minutes, being careful not to let it burn.

8 Transfer the stew to a warmed serving dish or bowl and serve.

Serve with a dense, smooth red wine with aromas of forest fruit such as Ribera del Duero.

1 kg (2¼ lb) boneless fresh leg of pork or pork shoulder

1 large yellow onion, thinly sliced

2 carrots, peeled and chopped

1 leek, white and pale green parts, chopped

2 ripe tomatoes, chopped

6 cloves garlic, peeled and crushed

½ lemon

8 black peppercorns

1 fresh thyme sprig

2 bay leaves

750 ml (1¼ pints) red wine

15 g (½ oz) unsalted butter

60 ml (2 fl oz) olive oil

750 ml (1¼ pints) beef stock, or as needed

Salt

1 small slice coarse country bread

1 tablespoon olive oil

6 blanched almonds; 4 hazelnuts, skinned (page 173); 4 walnuts; and 1 tablespoon pine nuts

30 g (1 oz) bitter chocolate

Handful of fresh flat-leaved parsley leaves

Makes 4 servings

COSTELLES DE XAI A LA LLOSA AMB OLI D'HERBES

Stone-cooked Lamb Chops with Herb Oil

A la llosa, literally "on the stone", refers to a technique for cooking meat on a flat stone placed over an open fire. The meat is briefly seared on a garlic-rubbed slab of slate, yielding tender and juicy results with a smoky aroma from the hot stone. The technique has been borrowed from farmhouses and rural kitchens, to appear on restaurant menus in Barcelona. You can re-create it with a cast-iron griddle or heavy frying pan, or better still, invest in a cooking stone like the Italian one made by Olare that fits into a metal frame with handles, enabling you to cook Pyrenean style directly at the table.

FOR THE HERB OIL

2 fresh sage leaves

1 bay leaf, crumbled

Leaves from 4 fresh flat-leaved parsley sprigs

Leaves from 3 fresh mint sprigs

Leaves from 3 fresh basil sprigs

Leaves from 1 fresh marjoram sprig

Leaves from 1 fresh oregano sprig

Leaves from 2 rocket sprigs

1 tablespoon chopped fresh chives

1 clove garlic, peeled

250 ml (8 fl oz) extra virgin olive oil

Salt and freshly ground pepper

1 clove garlic, halved

12 thin-cut lamb chops each about 85 g (3 oz) and 12 mm (½ inch) thick

Salt and freshly ground pepper

Lemon wedges for serving

Makes 6 servings

1 To make the herb oil, using a large mortar and pestle, grind together the sage, bay leaf, parsley, mint, basil, marjoram, oregano, rocket, chives, and garlic until a thick paste forms. Add the olive oil in a thin stream, continuing to mash the herbs, to make a bright green, fragrant sauce. Season to taste with salt and pepper.

2 Rub a griddle, frying pan, or cooking stone (see above) with the cut sides of the garlic halves. Heat the pan over high heat until sizzling hot. Season the lamb chops with salt and pepper. Working in batches, sear the chops briefly on both sides until just cooked through, about 2 minutes on each side. Be careful not to overcook the lamb, as it dries out easily.

3 Drizzle the chops with the herb oil and serve at once with the lemon wedges on the side.

Serve with a well-rounded, aromatic red wine from the Ribera del Duero.

ORADA A LA SAL
Whole Fish Baked in Salt

Packing a whole fish in rock salt is one of the best ways to cook it. The salt keeps the flesh moist and seems to lock in the flavour of the fish, while the skin acts as a barrier to lock out the intense saltiness. The whole fish emerging from its salty tomb is a spectacle in itself, but the real beauty of this dish is its total simplicity. You need serve nothing more alongside than a green vegetable – perhaps steamed green beans with butter – and new potatoes. If you like, pass a bowl of freshly made allioli (page 105) for guests to help themselves.

1 Preheat the oven to 245°C (475°F). Butter a baking dish large enough to hold the fish comfortably.

2 Place the fish in the prepared dish and cover evenly and completely with the rock salt. Bake until the salt has formed a hard crust, about 45 minutes.

3 Using a large stainless-steel spoon, remove as much of the salt as possible. Skin and fillet the fish carefully, and transfer the fillets to individual plates.

4 Season with a generous grinding of pepper and serve with the lemon wedges.

Serve with a fragrant, fruity white Albariño from Galicia or a Penedès white.

1 whole *dorada* (gilthead bream) or other firm-fleshed fish, about 1.35 kg (3 lb), cleaned and scaled by the fishmonger

1.8 kg (4 lb) rock salt

Freshly ground pepper

1 lemon, cut into wedges

Makes 4 servings

Salt

Salt plays an important role in the culinary and economic history of the Catalan lands. The coastal salt flats of Santa Pola and Torrevieja, and those on the island of Ibiza, have been a vital source of income at least since the days of the Phoenicians, who established the salt trade across the Mediterranean basin. The technique of encasing food, particularly seafood, in salt and then baking it originated in the salt-producing regions of the Alicante. As one of the most basic forms of food preservation, salt is still used in the production of Catalan hams and *embotits* (sausages) and in *bacallà,* salt cod. The fresh cod was brought by Catalan fishermen from Iceland and the Faroe Islands and is a perfect example of the use of salt as a preservative.

Salt is widely used in Spanish cuisine, and non-Spaniards often remark on the amount of salt used in the local cooking. Tapas, which are designed to accompany beer and wine, are often highly salted as an incentive to drink more. In fact, the local appetite for salty foods seems to be natural in a hot climate, where the body needs more of this vital substance.

FIDEUÀ

Vegetable and Seafood Noodles

According to legend, in the small port of Gandía, a fisherman was about to make a paella with the fish and shellfish he had just caught. Discovering he had no rice, he used pasta instead – and fideuà *was born. It is now one of the most popular dishes in the Catalan repertoire, and most restaurants along the old port of Barcelona include it on the menu. The name comes from* fideo *(*fideu *in Catalan), the generic term for pasta common all over Spain. In this case, it refers to a short, thin macaroni. As with paella, the success of* fideuà *depends largely on the quality of the stock. Serve with crusty country bread.*

225 g (8 oz) medium-size raw prawns in the shell

675 g (1½ lb) fish heads and bones

12 large mussels, about 450 g (1 lb) total weight

12 large cockles or clams in the shell, about 450 g (1 lb) total weight

4 ripe tomatoes, about 450 g (1 lb) total weight, cored

Sea salt

½ teaspoon saffron threads

120 ml (4 fl oz) olive oil

225 g (8 oz) mullet, grouper, or other firm-fleshed fish fillets, cut into 2.5 cm (1 inch) cubes

1 large red sweet pepper, seeded and cut into ½ inch (12 mm) dice

225 g (8 oz) *fideos* or other short, thin macaroni

4 cloves garlic, finely chopped

Handful of fresh flat-leaved parsley leaves, finely chopped

Makes 4–6 servings

1 In a stockpot over high heat, bring 1.25 l (2 pints) water to the boil. Meanwhile, peel the prawns and add the heads and shells to the water; set the peeled prawns aside. Add the fish heads and bones and return to the boil, skimming off any foam. Reduce the heat to medium-low and simmer gently, uncovered, until the liquid has reduced by one-third, about 30 minutes. Strain the liquid through a colander or sieve lined with muslin and placed over a bowl. Return the strained liquid to the stockpot.

2 Scrub the mussels and cockles with a stiff brush. Remove the mussel beards by scraping off the tuft of fibres with a knife. Pour water to a depth of 2.5 cm (1 inch) into a wide saucepan over medium-high heat. Add the mussels, discarding any that do not close to the touch, cover, and cook, shaking the pan occasionally, until they open, about 5 minutes. Using a slotted spoon, remove the mussels and discard any that have failed to open. Reserve the pan and water.

3 Using the same pan and water, cook the cockles in the same way and set aside. Strain the cooking water through a colander or sieve lined with muslin and add to the stockpot.

4 Halve the tomatoes, grate the flesh on the large holes of a grater-shredder into a bowl, and discard the skins. Set aside. Using a mortar and pestle, grind 1 teaspoon salt with the saffron until a deep yellow powder forms. Set aside.

5 In a 16 inch (40 cm) paella pan or wide, heavy frying pan over medium heat, warm the olive oil. Add the peeled prawns and cook, turning in the hot oil, until opaque throughout, about 1 minute. Transfer to a bowl with the slotted spoon. Cook the fish cubes in the same way until opaque, about 2 minutes. Transfer with the slotted spoon to the bowl with the prawns. Add the sweet pepper and fry until just soft, about 2 minutes, then transfer with the slotted spoon to the bowl with the prawns and fish.

6 Add the macaroni, garlic, and parsley to the pan and fry in the hot oil until fragrant and the macaroni is coated in oil, about 30 seconds. Add the tomato pulp, mixing well, and fry for 30 seconds longer. Pour in 1 l (1¾ pints) of the fish stock and add the prawns, fish, sweet pepper, and saffron mixture, stirring to distribute the ingredients evenly. Reduce the heat to low and simmer gently, without stirring, until almost all of the stock is absorbed by the macaroni, about 20 minutes. After the macaroni has been cooking for about 10 minutes, arrange the mussels and cockles or clams (in their shells) on the surface.

7 Turn off the heat and cover the pan with a clean kitchen towel. Let rest for about 10 minutes to allow the flavours to mingle thoroughly and the macaroni to absorb any remaining juices. Serve warm, not hot.

Serve with a slightly sparkling, crisp white wine.

POSTRES

Whether home-made or available at the neighbourhood *pastisseries*,

TRENCADENTS 2€

the sweet flavours of Barcelona offer something for everyone.

Spanish cuisine is not well known for desserts, but the more closely you look, the more variety and quality you will see. French-influenced pastries come together with traditional sweets from the Catalan kitchen to create a surprisingly wide dessert repertoire, from simple classics like *mel i mató* (fresh cheese with honey) to more complex preparations. It is quite acceptable in Barcelona to buy cakes, pastries, and biscuits from the *pastisseria,* although desserts, such as *crema catalana* and *flam,* are almost always homemade. Catalans appreciate locally grown fruit, and a selection of them makes an authentically Mediterranean finish to a meal.

MEL I MATÓ AMB FIGUES

Fresh Cheese and Honey with Figs

Mató is a fresh cheese no more than a day or two old. Pearly white, cool and creamy, with the taste of fresh milk, it is a cheese that is only just barely a cheese. Formerly made from goat's or sheep's milk, but now often from cow's milk, the best examples come from Montserrat, the mountain range outside Barcelona, and from the village of Fonteta, near Girona. The most widely available equivalent is probably ricotta, although any fresh curd cheese will work. Sprinkled with a little sugar, mató *is a favourite breakfast food throughout Catalonia.*

1 If using *mató,* cut the cheese into slices 2.5 cm (1 inch) thick and arrange on individual plates. Alternatively, if the cheese is not solid enough to slice, divide it evenly and spoon it on to each plate.

2 Using a small, sharp knife, remove the woody stems from the figs. Cut each fig into quarters longthways and arrange them, flesh side up, next to the cheese on each plate.

3 Drizzle the honey evenly over the cheese and figs and serve at once.

Serve with a golden, silky *moscatel* from Alicante.

450 g (1 lb) *mató* or whole-milk ricotta cheese

4–6 ripe figs, about 175 g (6 oz) total weight

175 g (6 oz) light, aromatic honey such as orange blossom

Makes 4 servings

Honey

The ancient Romans believed that the best honeys in the Mediterranean came from Greece. But the second-best honeys, they insisted, were from the Balearic Islands. Majorca and Ibiza still produce exquisite honey on a domestic scale, but the focus of the industry has shifted to other parts of Spain. Catalonia now claims over sixty-five thousand beehives, and areas like Port de Beseit in the south of the region and Pla de Bages in the north are known for their fragrant artisanal honeys.

The commonest type of honey in Catalonia is *milflores* (thousand flowers), followed by honeys derived from thyme, rosemary, and heather. But the most highly prized honey in Spain is *azahar*, or orange blossom honey, from the extensive orange groves outside Valencia.

Honey is used in unique ways in Catalan cooking; it turns up in *alberginies dolces*, aubergine fritters drizzled with honey, and is paired with almonds to make the Christmas nougat, *turrón*. Perhaps the oddest use is in *bacallà amb mel,* salt cod with honey, a medieval throwback of Catalan cuisine.

CREMA CATALANA

Catalan Burnt Cream

Crema catalana *is traditionally made for the feast of St Joseph on 16 March, but it is also an everyday delicacy enjoyed throughout the region. You'd be hard pressed to find a Barcelona restaurant menu that doesn't feature* crema catalana. *The bad news, given such popularity, is that it is a little tricky to make. The consistency of the custard must be neither too firmly set nor excessively liquid, but just solid enough to be eaten in deliciously creamy spoonfuls. Traditionally, a spiral iron is heated until extremely hot, then used to create the brittle sugar crust. A kitchen torch or gas grill can be substituted with excellent results.*

8 large egg yolks

175 g (6 oz) sugar

30 g (1 oz) cornflour

1 l (1¾ pints) full cream milk

Grated zest of ½ lemon

7.5 cm (3 inch) piece cinnamon stick

Makes 6 servings

1 In a bowl, using a balloon whisk, beat together the egg yolks and 125 g (4 oz) of the sugar until pale and creamy, about 6 minutes.

2 In a large bowl, dissolve the cornflour in 60 ml (2 fl oz) of the milk. In a heavy-bottomed saucepan over low heat, combine the rest of the milk, the lemon zest, and the cinnamon stick and heat until bubbles form along the edges of the pan, about 10 minutes.

3 Whisk the egg yolk mixture into the cornflour mixture until well blended. Add a little of the hot milk, whisking constantly to prevent the yolks from curdling. Add the remaining milk little by little while continuing to whisk.

4 Strain the mixture through a fine-meshed sieve back into the saucepan used for heating the milk. Heat slowly over very low heat, stirring constantly, until the mixture thickens into a custard, about 15 minutes. Do not let it boil or the mixture will curdle.

5 Pour the custard into six 250 ml (8 fl oz) shallow custard cups or ramekins or into a 2 l (3½ pint) capacity shallow gratin dish and let cool to room temperature. Cover with cling film and refrigerate until well chilled, at least 2 hours or up to 12 hours.

6 Make the sugar crust no more than 30 minutes before serving, or the topping will be soggy instead of crisp. Dust the surface of the cold custard evenly with the remaining sugar, dividing it evenly if using individual custard cups.

7 Using a kitchen torch, and holding it 5–7.5 cm (2–3 inches) from the surface, caramelise the sugar by constantly moving the flame over the top until the sugar bubbles. Alternatively, preheat a gas grill to maximum heat. Place the custard cups or gratin dish on a baking sheet and place under the grill 7.5 cm (3 inches) from the heat source. Grill until the top is caramelised, about 2 minutes. The burnt sugar should form a thin sheet of golden brown caramel.

Serve with an intense, richly flavoured *moscatel.*

POSTRE DEL MÚSIC
Musician's Dessert

The name of this dish alludes to the musicians of the cobal, *the wind instrument bands that played at the banquets of the medieval era. Els músics were commonly served with a bowl of fruit and nuts and a flagon of wine to keep up their strength. Nowadays "the musician's dessert" is brought out at the end of a meal or in the afternoon or early evening, when a few people might be gathered around the table for a chat and suddenly feel a little hungry. A glass or two of sweet wine is considered a mandatory accompaniment for this dessert.*

1 In a small frying pan over medium-high heat, toast the hazelnuts until the skins begin to darken and visibly loosen, about 3 minutes. Remove from the heat and rub off the skins with a clean, dry kitchen towel. Set aside to cool.

2 In the same pan over medium-high heat, toast the blanched almonds until golden brown, about 1 minute. Pour on to a plate to cool. In the same pan over medium-high heat, toast the walnuts until lightly coloured, about 1 minute. Pour on to a plate to cool.

3 Combine the cooled nuts and dried fruits in a serving dish, or arrange decoratively on individual plates before serving.

Serve with a *moscatel*, Malvasia, or other dessert wine.

75 g (2½ oz) hazelnuts

75 g (2½ oz) blanched almonds

60 g (2 oz) walnuts

340 g (12 oz) mixed dried fruits such as raisins, dates, prunes, figs, and apricots

Makes 6 servings

Dessert Wines

To satisfy their sweet tooth, Catalans like nothing better than a glass of sweet wine with dessert, in the afternoon with biscuits or cake, or even as a midday *aperitiu* (aperitif). The range of sweet wines in Catalonia is broad and complex, although none is made in large quantities. Most famous and characteristic are the *rancis* of Tarragona, a traditional style of highly alcoholic wine that is aged for a minimum of four years. *Vi ranci* is widely used in Catalan cooking.

The *vins dolços,* or sweet wines, of the Empordá, made with the Garnatxa grape, are also old-fashioned wines, relatively strong in alcohol and usually aged for two years or more in oak.

Malvasia de Sitges is a malmsey, one of the rarest wines in Spain, made in tiny quantities in the town of Sitges near Barcelona. It has a velvety richness nicely balanced with acidity that is reminiscent of orange marmalade. *Ratafia,* a speciality of Lleida and the surrounding *comarques* (counties), is an unusual treat: a sweet infusion of walnuts and spices, taken as an aperitif or post-prandial tipple. It was popular in England in Victorian times.

MONA DE XOCOLATA
Chocolate Truffle Cake

Come Easter time, a display of delicious cakes starts appearing in the windows of Barcelona pastisseries like Escribà and Fargas. From simple chocolate cakes to vast sculptures made entirely of chocolate, mona de Pasqua, Catalonia's Easter cake par excellence, takes a wide variety of forms. Nearly all modern mones are coated in some form of chocolate, and the grandest mones of all—those that hit the headlines in the local press—are positive works of art. This recipe, from Chocovic, Catalonia's dynamic chocolate company, falls half-way between an old-fashioned and a modern mona.

FOR THE CHOCOLATE CREAM

360 ml (12 fl oz) double cream

60 g (2 oz) sugar

140 g (5 oz) bitter chocolate, grated

FOR THE CAKE

285 g (10 oz) unsalted butter, at room temperature

6 large eggs, at room temperature

285 g (10 oz) sugar

285 g (10 oz) plain flour

FOR THE SYRUP

115 g (4 oz) sugar

250 ml (8 fl oz) water

200 g (7 oz) bitter chocolate, broken into small pieces

Miniature chocolate eggs (optional)

Makes 10–12 servings

1 To make the chocolate cream, in a small saucepan over low heat, bring the cream to a gentle simmer. Add the sugar and stir until dissolved. Add the grated chocolate and stir until the chocolate is melted. Let cool, then cover and refrigerate for 24 hours.

2 To make the sponge cake, preheat the oven to 190°C (375°F). Butter a 25 cm (10 inch) cake tin. Dust it with flour and tap out the excess.

3 In a bowl, cream the butter with a wooden spoon until pale and fluffy. In a separate bowl, using a hand-held mixer or balloon whisk, beat together the eggs and sugar until the mixture is pale and triples in volume. Add the butter a little at a time, beating constantly, until thoroughly combined. Sift the flour into the butter mixture and mix well.

4 Pour the batter into the prepared tin. Bake the cake until golden brown on top when a skewer inserted into the centre will come out clean, about 50 minutes. Transfer to a wire rack to cool.

5 To make the syrup, in a small saucepan, combine the sugar and water. Bring to the boil over medium heat and cook until a syrupy consistency forms, about 4 minutes. Do not let it turn golden. Remove from the heat and set aside to cool.

6 Place the chocolate pieces in the top pan of a double boiler or in a stainless-steel bowl. Set the pan or bowl over (not touching) barely simmering water in a saucepan. Heat until the chocolate melts, stirring occasionally. Do not allow any steam to come into contact with the chocolate. Alternatively, melt the chocolate in a microwave oven on defrost setting for 3 minutes.

7 Pour the chocolate on to a cool, smooth surface (ideally a marble or polished stone surface), allowing it to spread into a wafer-thin layer. Let cool completely. With a sharp, heavy knife, shave away the chocolate from the surface, forming delicate curls.

8 To assemble the cake, remove the chocolate cream from the refrigerator and beat with a hand-held mixer or balloon whisk until it is thick enough to spread with a knife. Using a large serrated knife, cut the sponge cake horizontally into 2 equal layers. Place the bottom half of the cake, cut side up, on a serving plate. Brush half the syrup over the cut side, then spread with about half the chocolate cream, creating a thick coating. Carefully place the top half of the cake, cut side up, over the chocolate cream and top it with the remaining syrup and then the remaining chocolate cream. Decorate the cake with the chocolate curls and with the chocolate eggs, if using.

Serve with a rich, plummy Port or other fortified dessert wine from the Penedès.

FLAÓ EIVISSENC

Ibiza Goat Cheese Tart with Mint

The culture on the island of Ibiza has much in common with Catalan culture; in fact, it is considered part of the països catalans, or Catalan lands. On one small farm, an elderly peasant lady named Maria kept a small herd of goats and made fresh cheese, which formed the basis of her superb flaó. Maria insisted on two ingredients in her flaó that made it into something special: a spoonful of aniseeds in the pastry dough and a sprinkling of fresh mint in the filling. The mint cuts the richness of the tart with a hint of freshness. You can substitute fresh cow's milk cheese instead, as it has a milder flavour.

1 To make the dough, sift the flour into a bowl. Make a well in the centre, and add the aniseeds, liqueur, and oil. Using your fingertips, lightly mix the flour with the other ingredients until the mixture resembles coarse breadcrumbs. Add 3 tablespoons of the water and continue to mix until you have a smooth, elastic dough, adding the remaining tablespoon of water if needed.

2 Butter a 23 cm (9 inch) tart or flan tin with a removable bottom. On a lightly floured work surface, roll out the dough into a 28 cm (11 inch) round about 6 mm (¼ inch) thick. Transfer the round to the prepared tart pan, pressing it smoothly against the bottom and sides. Trim the edges so they are even with the pan rim. Set the pastry-lined pan aside.

3 Preheat the oven to 180°C (350°F). To make the filling, in a bowl, lightly mash the cheese with a fork. Add the eggs, granulated sugar, and lemon zest. Tear the mint leaves into very small pieces and add to the bowl. Mix well and pour into the pastry shell.

4 Bake the tart until the top is pale gold, about 30 minutes. Transfer the tart to a wire rack and let cool completely. The filling may puff up slightly but will settle as it begins to cool.

5 Remove the pan sides and carefully slide the tart onto a plate. Using a fine-meshed sieve or sifter, dust the top of the tart with icing sugar, if using. Cut into wedges to serve.

Serve with a mahogany-coloured dessert wine made from the Pedro Ximénez grape.

FOR THE DOUGH

250 g (9 oz) plain flour

1 teaspoon aniseeds

60 ml (2 fl oz) anise liqueur such as *anis seco*, Pernod, or pastis

60 ml (2 fl oz) rapeseed or flavourless vegetable oil

60 ml (2 fl oz) water

Unsalted butter for greasing

FOR THE FILLING

450 g (1 lb) *mató* (page 60) or whole-milk ricotta cheese

4 large eggs, beaten

225 g (8 oz) granulated sugar

Grated zest of 1 lemon

4 fresh mint leaves

Icing sugar for dusting (optional)

Makes one 23 cm (9 inch) tart, or 6 servings

PA DE PESSIC AMB AVELLANES I REGALESSIA
Hazelnut Cake with Liquorice

Espai Sucre is a restaurant unlike any other in Barcelona, in Catalonia, or perhaps in the world: it serves only desserts. And what desserts! Chef Jordi Butrón trained with Ferran Adrià, the famed chef of the restaurant El Bulli in Roses, and has inherited something of the master's original take on ingredients, not to mention the scientific precision with which he works on his sweet creations. The following is Butrón's version of the classic Catalan sponge cake, or pa de pessic, *featuring toasted hazelnuts and a spoonful of ground liquorice, which gives the cake a delicious and aromatic kick.*

210 g (7½ oz) hazelnuts

4 large eggs, at room temperature

225 g (8 oz) granulated sugar

225 g (8 oz) unsalted butter, at room temperature

140 g (5 oz) plain flour

2 teaspoons ground liquorice (see Note)

Icing sugar for dusting (optional)

Makes 6 servings

1 Preheat the oven to 190°C (375°F). Butter a 25 cm (10 inch) cake tin. Dust with flour and tap out the excess.

2 In a small frying pan over medium-high heat, toast the hazelnuts until the skins begin to darken and visibly loosen, about 3 minutes. Remove from the heat and rub off the skins with a clean, dry kitchen towel. Put half the hazelnuts into a food processor and process just until it becomes a fine powder, being careful not to over-process. Wrap the remaining half of the hazelnuts in a clean, dry kitchen towel and gently break into pieces with a mallet.

3 In a bowl, using a whisk, beat together the eggs and granulated sugar until the mixture becomes a pale, creamy mousse and has tripled in volume, about 5 minutes. Add the butter little by little while continuing to whisk. Then add the flour, ground hazelnuts, hazelnut pieces, and liquorice and mix well.

4 Pour the batter into the prepared pan. Bake until a skewer inserted into the centre comes out clean, about 50 minutes. Let cool slightly on a wire rack. Run a table knife around the inside edge of the pan to loosen the cake, then invert the cake on to a serving plate. Using a fine-meshed sieve or sifter, dust the top of the cake with icing sugar, if using. Serve the cake warm or at room temperature.

Serve with a nutty, rich, full-bodied aged sherry.

Note: Ground liquorice powder can be found in speciality and wholefood shops, or it can be made by grinding dried liquorice root in a spice grinder or food processor.

GRANISSAT DE CAVA

"Liquid" Granita of Sparkling Wine

Barcelona is one of the most northerly of Spain's major cities, yet it has the climate of the southern Mediterranean. On some days in mid-summer, the temperature soars to 40°C (105°F) and higher, and the humidity can make the city feel sticky and uncomfortable. Barcelonans who can afford it disappear to the mountains for the entire month of August. Those who remain do their best to take life easy, with strolls along the old harbour in the evening, an afternoon dip in the sea at one of the city beaches, and a cooling granissat *any time of the day.*

1 Pour the wine into a shallow metal pan that will fit in the freezer. Freeze it, uncovered, until almost solid, about 3 hours.

2 Remove the pan from the freezer and break up the ice with a fork, scraping it from the sides of the pan. Add the sugar and the lemon zest and juice and mix thoroughly with a fork. If you prefer a sweeter taste, add more sugar. Return to the freezer for 1 hour.

3 Tear the mint leaves into very small pieces, add to the ice mixture, and mix again with a fork, breaking up the ice mixture into small crystals. Spoon into tall glasses and let stand for about 10 minutes to melt slightly. By the time you serve the granita, it should be just liquid enough to drink through a straw.

1 bottle (750 ml/24 fl oz) good-quality dry *cava* or other brut sparkling wine

2 tablespoons sugar, or more as needed

Finely grated zest and juice of 1 lemon

4–6 fresh mint leaves

Makes 4–6 servings

Cava

Cava is Spain's celebration wine, popular at Christmas and New Year celebrations when it is accompanied by *turróns* and other sweets at the end of a festive meal. Until recently, *cava* had a reputation as "poor man's fizz" and was usually thin and acidic. Since the 1990s, however, it has improved remarkably. It is now one of the better sparkling wines on the international market and offers superb value for the money.

The best-known *cava* producers are found in Catalonia, where almost eleven million cases are made annually from the local varieties of white grape, using the *methode champenoise.* The grape stocks used are Macabeo, Parellada, and Xarello, plus Chardonnay from the New World. Depending on the degree of sweetness, *cava* may be described on the bottle as *extra-brut, brut, brut nature, extra seco, seco, semi-seco,* or *dulce.* Among the best-known producers of *cava* are Juvé i Camps, Codorníu, Freixenet, and Segura Viudas.

An annual Festa del Cava is held in October in the town of Sant Sadurní d'Anoia, the capital of *cava* production.

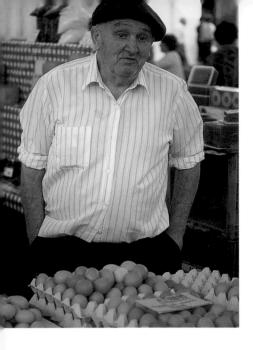

FLAM

Crème Caramel

Flam (or flan in Spanish) is a dish whose popularity in Spain cuts across all borders. You can hardly avoid coming across it at some point during a stay in Barcelona, especially if you happen to visit one of the hundreds of bars and restaurants offering a reasonably priced menú del día. The wobbly milk-and-egg custard with a crown of caramel is one of the most memorable finishes to a meal. It is normally prepared in individual metal pots known as flaneras, specially made for the purpose. Since they can be difficult to find outside Spain, individual-sized ramekins or small custard cups may be substituted.

3 tablespoons sugar, plus 225 g (8 oz)

2 tablespoons water

600 ml (1 pt) full cream milk

1 vanilla bean, split lengthways, or a few drops of vanilla extract

2 large whole eggs plus 6 egg yolks

Makes 6 servings

1 In a small saucepan, combine the 3 tablespoons sugar and the water. Bring to a boil over medium heat and boil, without stirring, until the mixture becomes a golden brown syrup, about 4 minutes.

2 Pour an equal amount of the caramel syrup into each of six 125 ml (4 fl oz) *flaneras,* ramekins, or custard cups, tipping and rotating the moulds until the sides are coated about halfway up.

3 Pour the milk into a saucepan, add the vanilla bean, and place over low heat until small bubbles appear along the edge of the pan, about 7 minutes. Do not allow the milk to boil.

4 Preheat the oven to 150°C (300°F). In a bowl, using a balloon whisk, beat together the eggs, egg yolks, and the rest of the sugar until a pale, creamy mousse forms. Add a little of the hot milk, whisking constantly to prevent the yolks from curdling. Add the remaining milk little by little while continuing to whisk. Strain the custard through a fine-meshed sieve into the prepared moulds, dividing it evenly.

5 Place the filled moulds in a large baking dish and carefully add boiling water to reach halfway up the sides of the moulds.

6 Bake the custards until they are set but the centres still jiggle just slightly, 50–60 minutes. Touch the surface of the custard lightly with the point of a knife; it should come away cleanly when set. Remove the baking dish from the oven and lift the moulds out of the water. Let cool to room temperature, then cover and refrigerate until well chilled, at least 2 hours or up to 6 hours.

7 To serve, run a sharp, thin knife blade around the inside of each mould and unmould the custards on to individual plates.

Serve with a light, honeyed dessert wine from Navarre.

GLOSSARY

ALLIOLI This pale, pungent sauce gets its heady flavour from raw garlic and its thickness from olive oil. Much loved in Spain, it is often served as a dip or sauce for fish, shellfish, meat, vegetables, or rice dishes. It is traditionally prepared with a mortar and pestle and may include honey, nuts, herbs, or puréed fruit such as quince, apple, or pear.

ANCHOVIES See page 49.

ANISEED The anise plant, a member of the parsley family, has feathery leaves and small, crescent-shaped seeds that boast a sweet liquorice flavour. Used both whole and ground, the seeds add their distinctive taste to breads, pastries, and biscuits.

ANISE LIQUEUR A strongly flavoured distilled spirit enjoyed throughout southern Europe, where it is produced under various names, including *anis seco* in Spain, pastis or Pernod in France, *ouzo* in Greece, and *anesone* in Italy. Infused with the liquorice-like flavour of green aniseed, the liqueur is used in cooking and drunk as an aperitif.

ASPARAGUS Early spring brings the first wild asparagus spears (sprü) to open air markets, an eagerly awaited event all across Spain. The long stalks are actually the shoots of a plant of the lily family, harvested while still young and tender. Most arrive at market bright green in colour, varying from slender pencil-sized stems to jumbo stalks 2 cm (¾ inch) thick. White asparagus is grown away from light to blanch it to a pale ivory colour and create a more delicate flavour. Wash asparagus spears in plenty of cool water to remove any sand in the tips.

BOTIFARRA See page 40.

BROAD BEANS From spring into summer, gardens throughout Spain yield profuse crops of broad beans. As the long, wide pods grow older, the inner skin on each bean thickens. Select small pods for the tenderest broad beans, and blanch older beans to help in removing their tough skins.

CANSALADA The dry mountain air of northern Catalonia is well suited for preserving foods, a factor that has contributed to making the region a celebrated source of the charcuterie that plays an important role in Spanish cuisine as a whole. Literally "salted meat", *cansalada* is the local version of bacon. Any cured fatty bacon, in particular green (unsmoked) bacon, can be used in its place.

CASSOLA The thick walls of this round, shallow earthenware pan, also known as a *cazuela*, allow foods to cook gently and evenly. Ideal for long, slow cooking in the oven, the orange terracotta of a *cassola* is traditionally glazed only on the inside surface. Season a new *cassola* by immersing it in water for 6 hours. Repeat this soaking occasionally if you live in a dry climate or if you plan to use the pan over the direct flame of a hob (although it is not recommended for use on the hob). To prevent cracks, do not heat the pan while it is empty, limit the temperature to very low for its use on the stove top, and avoid temperature extremes.

CHESTNUTS These treasured nuts grow in the regions surrounding the Pyrenees, where during the autumn months, you can purchase the fresh, hot, starchy-sweet delicacies from street-sellers. Cooked and canned chestnuts are available, but fresh ones are worth the extra bit of work needed to remove the tough mahogany-coloured shells.

SHELLING CHESTNUTS: To remove the shells, cut a shallow X into the flat side of each nut, then immerse them in boiling water or roast them in a 180°C (350°F) oven for about 15 minutes. Working with a few nuts at a time while keeping the others warm, peel back the points of the X to remove the flesh. Peel off the thin beige inner skin and discard. If any nuts cool before you peel them, simply return them to the hot oven or water until their shells warm and soften again.

CHICK-PEAS These nutrient-rich pulses are a staple in many Mediterranean cuisines. The round, beige beans are rich and nutty in flavour, and their firm texture holds up well to long cooking. Rinse and drain canned chick-peas before using.

CHORIZO There are countless variations on this distinctive Iberian sausage. Made of air-dried pork and heavily spiced with garlic and paprika, chorizo has a rich, smoky-sweet flavour with a hint of tanginess. Each region has its own special style, which may be mild or spicy, fresh or cured, air-dried or wood-smoked. There are two basic categories of chorizo: sausages meant for cooking and those cured for eating uncooked, although some versions can be eaten both hot and cold. In the kitchen, chorizo is most often used in small amounts as a flavouring, adding depth to stocks, sauces, fillings, tortillas, eggs, and bean dishes. Versions from Spain tend not to be as spicy-hot as Mexican-style chorizo, but the latter may be used as a substitute.

COCA, COQUES Small, pizza-like savoury pastries that are a speciality of the Costa Blanca and the Balearic Islands south of Barcelona. *Coques* feature a variety of toppings such as tomatoes and sweet peppers, olive oil and anchovies, aubergine, or dark greens and caramelised onions.

COGNAC A brandy distilled from grapes grown specifically in the district of Cognac in France. Aged a minimum of 2 years in oak casks, cognac brightens the flavour of pâtés and is often used to flambé stew meat after browning.

EMBOTITS Cold meats that have been cured according to Spain's long tradition of artisanal charcuterie. Highlighting the central role pork plays in the country's cuisine, a selection of *embotits* might include a pork loin cured with peppercorns, a finely textured ham, paprika sausage, or a special Catalan blood sausage (see page 40).

ENDIVE Pleasantly bitter in flavour, members of the endive family of greens take well to heartier salads and light cooking. Batavian endive has wide, flat leaves and pale white stalks loosely gathered around a green-yellow heart. It can be chopped and tossed in a salad or stirred into soups and pasta sauces. Curly endive, a close cousin of Batavian endive, has narrow, spiky, finely curled leaves and a creamy white heart. With its more delicate texture, it appears primarily in salads tossed with a simple vinaigrette. Although available year-round, both are at their peak during the winter season. Select crisp, compact heads free of any wilting or discolouration.

ENTREPÀ, ENTREPANS Literally "between bread", an *entrepà* is the Catalan interpretation of Spain's much-loved *bocadillo* sandwich. Traditionally enjoyed as a snack during the afternoon or late at night, *entrepans* are popular fare in bars and snack bars. Most *entrepans* have simple fillings such as *tortilla de patatas,* a basic egg omelette, fresh goat's cheese, or spicy chorizo sausage.

FIDEO Called *fideu* in Catalonia, the only region in Spain where pasta is widely used, these very thin, vermicelli-like noodles appear in a local version of paella. Fideo is also used in a variety of soups, stews, and vegetable dishes. Look for small bags of the pasta in Spanish grocers, or use the thinnest possible Itaian angel hair pasta you can find, broken into short lengths.

FISH The coastline of southern Catalonia allows easy access to the Mediterranean's abundant fish and seafood.

GROUPER Called *mero* in Spanish and *anfós* in Catalan, this fish thrives in the sea's warm waters. A thick-bodied fish with firm, flaky meat, grouper is superb roasted, grilled, or gently braised.

MONKFISH Often compared to lobster for its rich, white, firm, finely textured flesh, monkfish is prized by Spanish cooks. Called *rape* or *rap* in Spanish, it is excellent poached, grilled, or barbecued.

JAMÓN SERRANO See page 40.

MAHÓN See page 60.

MATÓ See page 60.

MONGETES DEL GANXET Large, white, kidney-shaped beans prized in Catalonia for their smooth texture and thin, delicate skins. The beans absorb flavour well when cooked with sausage, ham, rabbit, or lamb. Look for jars of *mongetes del ganxet* in Spanish grocers, or substitute with cannellini, haricot, or flageolet beans.

MORTAR AND PESTLE Many aromatic ingredients, such as garlic, release more of their oils when crushed in a pestle using a mortar than when chopped in a food processor or blender. Look for a generously sized marble or stone bowl when selecting a mortar, to allow easier and more efficient crushing. A proper *allioli* or *romesco* sauce, some Catalans would insist, is best served right in the rough-hewn mortar in which it was made.

MOSCATEL Also called muscat; see page 57.

NYORA PEPPERS Also known as *ñora* peppers, these are essential in an authentic *romesco* sauce. Grown mainly in Catalonia, plum-sized *nyora* peppers lend their red colour, sweet flavour, and mildly spicy heat to numerous local dishes. To prepare the dried peppers, cover with boiling water and soak for 10 minutes, then scrape the flesh from inside the skins. Dried ancho chilli peppers can be substituted.

PAELLA PAN Spain's famous rice dish is traditionally cooked outdoors in a wide, shallow metal pan placed over a fast-burning wood fire. A paella pan is made of rolled steel and sports two round handles. It can measure from 25 cm (10 inches) to more than 1 m (3 feet) across. A 30 or 35 cm (12 or 14 inch) pan can easily hold three to four generous servings. Paella pans should be seasoned and cleaned like woks and cast-iron pans. Avoid using soap when washing, dry thoroughly, and then coat with a thin film of oil before storing.

PANCETA Made from the thin, flat belly cut of pork, *panceta* is a streaky bacon often used in the beginning of cooking to flavour sauces, soups, and stews. Substitute Italian pancetta or any other green (unsmoked) bacon.

PARMA HAM This air-dried, salted ham has long been a speciality of Parma, a province of northern Italy. Made from pigs raised on a diet of chestnuts and whey, the finely textured ham has a sweet, nutty flavour much like Spain's serrano ham.

PASTISSERIA, PASTELERÍA For a mid-morning or afternoon *merienda* snack, Spaniards will visit a bakery to savour tea or coffee with one of their favourite sweets. Named *pastisseria* in Catalan and *pastelería* in Spanish, each bakery or patisserie offers a delectable selection of sweet and savoury snacks, including breads, pastries, and sweetmeats.

PASTIS See anise liqueur.

PÂTÉ A classic appetiser in France, pâté is essentially seasoned minced meat cooked gently in a fat-lined terrine or inside a pastry crust. Its texture can vary from coarsely chopped mixtures, known as country-style pâtés, to silky-smooth spreads.

PERNOD See anise liqueur.

PICADA A Catalan sauce based on ground nuts, typically almonds or hazelnuts. Thickened with toast and flavoured with garlic, saffron, paprika, parsley, vinegar, or wine, a picada gives rich body and depth of flavour when stirred into a stew. Some include unsweetened chocolate like the Mexican *mole.*

PIMENTÓN Spanish paprika, finely ground from dried nyora peppers (see left), can be sweet, bittersweet, or spicy hot. Look for pimentón in small tins in Spanish or speciality grocers, or use sweet paprika in its place.

PINE NUTS The small, pale seeds of certain varieties of pine trees have an elongated, tapered shape and a rich, sweet, slightly resinous flavour. Used often in southern European and Middle Eastern cooking, pine nuts appear in savoury dishes such as salads, stuffings, and sauces as well as in cakes, pastries, and desserts. Toast them for about 10 minutes in a 165°C (325°F) oven to bring out their nutty flavour.

PORT A sweet fortified wine produced by adding brandy to partially fermented red wine. Neighbouring Portugal, most notably the Douro Valley, produces the most renowned port wines, although port-style wines are also made in many other countries. Single-year vintage ports are the finest. Pale tawny ports, blended from several vintages, may be aged in wood for up to 40 years and are good for both drinking and cooking. Ruby ports, generally the least expensive, are aged in wood for 2–3 years.

QUESO FRESCO DE BURGOS A fresh sheep's milk cheese produced in Castile-Leon, a province in northern Spain. Made in 1 to 3 kg (2¼ to 6½ lb) cylinders and often including some cow's milk, this very fresh, rindless cheese, mild in flavour and white in colour, is very popular served with fruit for breakfast all across Spain.

RIBEIRO A wine region located in rugged, rainy Galicia, in the northwestern corner of Spain. Ribeiro's vineyards produce fresh, light white wines that are nearly always served young, within 2 years of bottling, to accompany fish and seafood.

RICE Brought to Spain by the Moors, rice became an important crop in the marshlands of southern Spain, where short-grain varieties thrive. Calasparra and Valencia rice, medium-short-grain varieties, and Bomba rice are still considered the best for paella.

Connoisseurs of Spanish rice refer to its *perla*, the pearl of starch at each grain's core that soaks up the flavours of other ingredients. Italian Arborio or Carnaroli rice is the closest equivalent.

ROCKET This delicate leafy green has a peppery, slightly bitter flavour that adds complexity to salads. Its assertive flavour and bright green colour also make it a favourite addition to sauces and soups. Look for small, crisp leaves that show no wilting or yellowing.

ROMESCO A classic Catalan dipping sauce thickened with almonds, olive oil, and bread. Wine vinegar and garlic round out its flavours, while local *nyora* peppers lend a red colour and a touch of heat. Some versions include hazelnuts, pine nuts, tomatoes, or spicy chilli peppers. Rich and pungent *romesco* accompanies a wide range of dishes, such as roast potatoes, seafood, rabbit, asparagus, or grilled spring onions.

SAFFRON Known as *azafrán* in Spain, this spice takes its name from the Arabic word for "yellow", evoking the bright hue it lends to dishes. Saffron threads, the dried stigmas of the purple autumn crocus, are still gathered by hand, one reason the spice is comparatively rare and costly. Introduced to Iberia by the Moors, it has become a signature seasoning in Spanish dishes, particularly paella.

SALCHICHÓN See page 41.

SARSUELA Also called *zarzuela*, this seafood speciality is served along the Catalan coast. Cooks combine a variety of fish and shellfish – whatever is particularly fresh on any given day – and add wine, tomatoes, saffron or paprika, and ground almonds or breadcrumbs to make a well-flavoured stew.

SERRANO HAM See page 40.

SHERRY Sherry takes its name from its place of origin, Jerez, a region of south-west Spain where Phœnician settlers first introduced grape vines. Blended and fortified, sherry wines fall into several styles. Dry or very dry *fino* has a straw colour and a delicate flavour that makes it ideal for tapas. Manzanilla, a lighter, bitter wine, is *fino* produced in the seaside town of Sanlúcar de Barrameda. It pairs with shellfish particularly well. Amber-hued Amontillado is a medium-dry wine with a rich, nutty

flavour that complements smoked meat and cheese. Medium-sweet Oloroso develops a dark mahogany colour and walnut flavour; serve it with sausages, nuts, or dried fruit. Sweet cream sherry is a dessert wine in Spain though elsewhere it is drunk as an aperitif.

SOBRASSADA See page 41.

SOFREGIT Many Catalan recipes start with this basic preparation. Although Catalan cooks add ingredients such as tomatoes, sweet peppers, garlic, carrots, or paprika, the essential combination remains that of onions and olive oil. *Sofregit* adds a distinctive sweet-savoury flavour to Catalan cuisine. Other regions of Spain refer to it as *sofrito*.

SQUID See page 48.

SUQUET A traditional Catalan seafood stew. One of the most popular versions combines fish, cockles, potatoes, and tomatoes in a broth that has been thickened with ground almonds and flavoured with paprika.

TOMATOES Tomatoes were first cultivated in Spain during the early sixteenth century. In Spanish kitchens, the narrow, firm plum tomato predominates, for its deeper flavour and its ability to withstand long cooking.

PEELING AND SEEDING TOMATOES: Cut a shallow X in the blossom end of the tomato. Immerse in a pan of boiling water until the peel begins to curl away from the X, about 30 seconds. Transfer to a bowl of ice water to cool, then peel away the skin. To seed, cut in half crossways and squeeze each half gently to dislodge the seeds.

TUNA When buying canned tuna for Spanish dishes, look for imported albacore tuna packed in olive oil. Its richer flavour and texture are essential in preparing certain dishes from southern Europe. If imported tuna is not available, use white albacore tuna packed in water. After draining it well, drizzle 2–3 tablespoons of extra virgin olive oil over the tuna and set aside for 5 minutes.

VI RANCI See page 57.

INGREDIENT SOURCES

EL CELLER CATALÀ

Catalan *cava*, white, and red wines, including Penedés, Priorat, Montsant, and Alella.

+ 34 977 638436

www.wwwinecellar.com

EL PANTAR

Arroz Bomba Illa de Riu is the highest quality Spanish rice, produced in limited quantities and much sought after by Spanish chefs.

+ 34 977 450594; + 34 977 451711 (fax)

email: elpantar@teleline.es

FORMATGERIA LA SEU

Artisan cheeses from Catalonia.

+ 34 93 412 65 48

www.formatgerialaseu.com

IGOURMET.COM

Spanish cheeses, chorizo, olive oil, ham, and rice.

(877) 446-8763

www.igourmet.com

BRINDISA

Spanish food, wine, and cookware, including Catalan cheeses, *nyora* peppers, *botifarra* sausages, serrano ham, chorizo, beans, vinegars, olive oils, paella pans, and terra-cotta *cassolas*. 32 Exmouth Market, Clerkenwell, London EC1 (020 7713 1666), and the Floral Hall, Borough Market, London SE1 (020 7407 1036)

CATALONIAN FOOD AND WINE

Spanish Embassy Office for Economic and Commercial Affairs - Second Floor - 66 Chiltern St. - W1U 4LS - London. Email: londres@mcx.es

Tel +44 207 467 2360

WWW.SPANISH-FIESTAS.COM/WINE/BARCELONA.HTM

Barcelonas wine tours

INDEX

A

Alella, 56

Allioli, 105, 185

Almonds
    musician's dessert, 173
    and pine nut biscuits, 80
    romesco, 121
    toasting, 173

Anchovies, 49, 79
    curly endive salad with salt cod, olives, and, 109
    sandwiches with fresh cheese, roasted sweet peppers, and, 79

Aniseed, 185

Anise liqueur, 185

Aperitiu, 87

Asparagus
    about, 185
    garlic and spring vegetable soup, 106

Aubergine, 102
    flatbread with sweet peppers, olives, and, 76
    roasted vegetable salad, 118
    salt cod with sweet peppers, onion, tomato, and, 141
    stuffed, 102

B

Bacallà. See Salt cod

Beans. *See also* Chick-peas; Broad beans
    mongetes del ganxet, 186
    two-course mixed stew of meat, vegetables, and, 153

Béchamel sauce, 129

Beef, braised, with mushrooms, 138

Beer, 87

Berberechos, 37

Biscuits, almond and pine nut, 80

Bonbons, 68, 69

La Boqueria, 25–26

Boquerones en vinagre, 36

Botifarres, 39, 40

Bread
    flat-, with aubergine, sweet peppers and olives, 76
    sandwiches with fresh cheese, anchovies and roasted sweet peppers, 79
    tomato-rubbed, 75

Broad beans, 186
    Catalan-style, 113
    garlic and spring vegetable soup, 106

Bull, 41

C

Cabbage
    mashed potatoes and, 114
    and pork bundles, 130

Cabra amb pebre, 61

Cakes
    chocolate truffle, 174
    hazelnut, with liquorice, 178

Calamars, 36, 48

Calçots, 121

Caldereta, 142

Cannelloni, feast-day, 129

Cansalada, 185

Cargols, 37

Cassola, 185

Catalana, 41

Cava, 56, 181

Chardonnay, 56

Cheese
    and honey with figs, 169
    making, 58
    sandwiches with anchovies roasted sweet peppers, and, 79
    shops, 58
    tart, Ibiza goat, with mint, 177
    varieties of, 60–61, 186

Chestnuts
    roast duck with raisins and, 154
    shelling, 185

Chicken
    baked rice with sausage, chick-peas, and, 145
    braised, with prawns, 149
    feast-day cannelloni, 129
    and ham croquettes, 92
    roasted, with garlic, 146

Chick-peas, 185
    baked rice with chicken, sausage, and, 145
    two-course mixed stew of beans, meat, and vegetables, 153

Chocolate, 66–69
    bonbons, 68, 69
    cream, 174
    truffle cake, 174

Chorizo, 185

Clams
    berberechos, 37
    vegetable and seafood noodles, 162

Cockles
    berberechos, 37
    vegetable and seafood noodles, 162

Cognac, 185

Coques, 64, 185
    de llardons, 65
    de recapte, 76
    de vidre, 91

Crema catalana, 170

Crème caramel, 182

Croquetas, 37

Croquettes, chicken and ham, 92

Cuisine, Catalan
    contemporary, 15–16, 19
    by geographical area, 27–29
    history of, 13–15
    influences on, 15–16, 83, 101, 129

Curly endive salad with salt cod, anchovies, and olives, 109

Custards
    Catalan burnt cream, 170
    crème caramel, 182

D

Dessert wines, 173

Duck, roast, with raisins and chestnuts, 154

E

Eggs
    spinach omelette with tomato sauce, 126

Embotits, 39, 41, 185

Empanada, 84

Entrepans, 79, 186

Escabetx, 88

Escalivada, 118

Escamarlans, 48

Escórpora, 49

Escudella, 153

Esqueixada de bacallà, 36

Endive, curly 185

F

Feast-day cannelloni, 129

Fideo, 186

Fideuà, 162

Fiestas, food-related, 109, 121

Figs, fresh cheese and honey with, 169

Fish. *See also* Anchovies; Monkfish; Salt cod;
　Sardines; Tuna
　shellfish and mixed meat paella, 137
　species of, 49, 186
　vegetable and seafood noodles, 162
　whole, baked in salt, 161

Flam, 182

Formatge de cabra enoli d'oliva, 61

Fuet, 40

G

Garlic and spring vegetable soup, 106

Garrotxa, 61

Gazpacho, 101

Granita, "liquid", of sparkling wine, 181

Grouper, 186

H I

Ham
　Catalan salad, 122
　and chicken croquettes, 92
　feast-day cannelloni, 129
　varieties of, 37, 40, 186

Hazelnuts
　cake with liquorice, 178
　musician's dessert, 173
　romesco, 121
　toasting, 173

Herb oil, 158

Honey
　about, 169
　and fresh cheese with figs, 169

Ibiza goat cheese tart with mint, 177

L

Lamb chops, stone-cooked, with herb oil, 158

Lentil soup, cream of, with garlic-herb croutons, 125

Llonganissa, 39, 41

Lobster soup, 142

M

Mahón, 60

Majorcan summer salad, 105

Map, 30–31

Mar i muntanya, 149

Markets, 25–26

Mató, 60

Meals. *See also individual meats*
　mixed, and shellfish paella, 137
　mixing seafood and, 149
　two-course mixed stew of beans, vegetables,
　　and, 153

Mercat de Sant Josep, 25–26

Mona, 174

Mongetes del ganxet, 186

Monkfish, 186
　medallions, thyme soup with, 110
　shellfish and mixed meat paella, 137

Mortar and pestle, 186

Moscatels, 54, 57

Mushrooms, 117
　braised beef with, 138
　oven-roasted wild, with garlic and parsley, 117

Musician's dessert, 173

Mussels, 48
　shellfish and mixed meat paella, 137
　vegetable and seafood noodles, 162

O

Oils
　herb, 158
　olive, 43–45

Olives
　curly endive salad with salt cod, anchovies,
　　and, 109
　flatbread with aubergines, sweet peppers, and, 76
　harvesting, 44
　oil, 43–45
　spicy marinated, with pickled vegetables and
　　garlic, 87

Omelette, spinach, with tomato sauce, 126

Onions, grilled spring, with *romesco* sauce, 121

Orada, 49

P

Pa amb tomàquet, 75

Paella
　pans, 186
　shellfish and mixed meat, 137

Panceta, 186
　Catalan-style broad beans, 113
　country-style pâté, 83
　mashed potatoes and cabbage, 114

Panellets, 80

Pasta
　feast-day cannelloni, 129
　fideo, 186
　two-course mixed stew of beans, meat
　　and vegetables, 153
　vegetable and seafood noodles, 162

Pastisseries, 62–65, 186

Patatas bravas, 36

Pâté
　about, 186
　country-style, 83

Peaches, pork loin with, 150

Peas
　garlic and spring vegetable soup, 106
　shellfish and mixed meat paella, 137

Penedès wines, 56, 57

Peppers
　flatbread with aubergine, olives, and, 76
　Majorcan summer salad, 105
　nyora, 186
　roasted vegetable salad, 118
　roasting, 79
　salt cod with aubergine, onion, tomato, and, 141
　sandwiches with fresh cheese, anchovies, and, 79
　and tuna pie, 84

Pernil ibéric, 37

Pernil salat, 40

Picada
　about, 13, 19, 186
　recipes, 117, 126, 157

Pimentón, 186

Pine nuts, 186
　and almond cookies, 80
　sweet pastry with, 91
　toasting, 186

Potatoes
  mashed, and cabbage, 114
  patatas bravas, 36
Prawns, 48, 95
  braised chicken with, 149
  griddled, with garlic and parsley, 95
  shellfish and mixed meat paella, 137
  vegetable and seafood noodles, 162
Priorat, 57

Q–R

Queso fresco de Burgos, 186
Raisins
  musician's dessert, 173
  roast duck with chestnuts and, 154
Restaurants
  with authentic Catalan cooking, 20
  by geographical area, 27–29
  noted, 14, 19, 20
  seafood, 23, 25
  trend-setting, 23, 27
  variety of, 14–15, 19–20
Ribeiro wines, 187
Rice, 187
  baked, with chicken, sausages,
    and chick-peas, 145
  shellfish and mixed meat paella, 137
Rioja, 56
Rocket, 185
Romesco, 121, 187

S

Saffron, 187
Salads
  Catalan, 122
  curly endive, with salt cod, anchovies,
    and olives, 109
  Majorcan summer, 105
  roasted vegetable, 118
Salchichón, 39, 41
Salt, 161
Salt cod, 36, 46, 141
  with aubergine, sweet peppers, onion,
    and tomato, 141
  curly endive salad with anchovies,
    olives, and, 109
Samfaina, 141
Sandwiches with fresh cheese, anchovies,
  and roasted sweet peppers, 79

Sardines
  about, 49
  fried, in vinaigrette, 88
Sarsuela, 46, 187
Sausage
  baked rice with chicken, chick-peas, and, 145
  Catalan salad, 122
  Catalan-style broad beans, 113
  varieties of, 39, 40, 41, 185
Seafood. *See also individual seafood*
  importance of, 46
  mixing meat and, 149
  restaurants, 23, 25
  shellfish and mixed meat paella, 137
  varieties of, 48–49
  and vegetable noodles, 162
Sherry, 187
Snacks, 34, 91
Sobrassada, 41
Sofregit, 130, 187
Soups
  cream of lentil, with garlic-herb croutons, 125
  garlic and spring vegetable, 106
  gazpacho, 101
  lobster, 142
  thyme, with monkfish medallions, 110
Spinach omelette with tomato sauce, 126
Squid, 36, 48
Stone-cooked lamb chops with herb oil, 158
Suau de Clua, 61
Suquet, 46, 187
Sweet peppers
  flatbread with aubergine, olives, and, 76
  Majorcan summer salad, 105
  nyora, 186
  roasted vegetable salad, 118
  roasting, 79
  salt cod with aubergine, onion, tomato, and, 141
  sandwiches with fresh cheese, anchovies, and, 79
  and tuna pie, 84

T

Tapas, 34, 36–37, 73, 101
Tart, Ibiza goat cheese, with mint, 177
Thyme soup with monkfish medallions, 110
Tomatoes, 187
  Catalan salad, 122
  gazpacho, 101
  Majorcan summer salad, 105

peeling and seeding, 187
roasted vegetable salad, 118
romesco, 121
-rubbed bread, 75
salt cod with aubergine, sweet peppers,
  onion, and, 141
sauce, spinach omelette with, 126
shellfish and mixed meat paella, 137
stuffed aubergine, 102
sweet pepper and tuna pie, 84
vegetable and seafood noodles, 162
Tou dels Tillers, 60
Trempó, 105
Trinxat, 114
Tuna, 187
  curly endive salad with salt cod, anchovies,
    and olives, 109
  and sweet pepper pie, 84

V

Veal
  stuffed aubergine, 102
Vegetables. *See also individual vegetables*
  salad, roasted, 118
  and seafood noodles, 162
  spring, 113
  spring, and garlic soup, 106
  two-course mixed stew of beans,
    meat, and, 153
Vi ranci, 57

W

Walnuts
  musician's dessert, 173
  toasting, 173
Wine bars, 52
  Wines. *See also* Port; Sherry
  DOs for, 52
  history of, 50–52, 55
  making, 54, 55
  sparkling, "liquid" granita of, 181
  varieties of, 52, 56–57, 173, 181, 187
Wine shops, 52

X

Xató, 109

ACKNOWLEDGMENTS

Paul Richardson would like to thank Edwina Taeger, Marc Taeger, Ana Valls, Joan Graells, Juan Ignacio Trives, Maria Teresa Pire, Marlena Spieler, Pepa Aymamí, Pep Palau, Christian Escribà, Jordi Alzina, all the folks at La Boqueria market, and the people of Barcelona in general for their helpfulness and good humour. *Gràcies a tothom!*

Weldon Owen wishes to thank the following individuals and organisations for their kind assistance: Desne Ahlers, Quentin Bacon, Dan Becker, Carrie Bradley, Brooke Buchanan, Ken DellaPenta, Elisabet der Nederlanden, George Dolese, Jean-Blaise Hall, Karen Kemp, Celeste Carrasco Moreno, Joan Olson, Scott Panton, Gilles Poidevin, Eric Ryan, Sharon Silva, and Karin Skaggs.

Weldon Owen would also like to extend their gratitude to the individuals and the owners and workers of restaurants, bakeries, shops, and other culinary businesses in Barcelona and Catalonia who participated in this project: Abac, Barceloneta restaurant, Bar del Pi, Bar Pinotxo, Boix de Cerdanya, Botifarreria de Santa Maria, Brunells, Cal Estevet, Cal Isidre, Cal Pep, Cansaladeria Alsina, Carme Butí, Carmelitas, Clara Guasch, Clos d' l'Obac winery, Comerç 24, DAF, El Celler Vell, El Xampanyet, El Nou Celler, Els Pescadors, El Taller, Escribà, Espai Sucre, Estrella de Plata, Eulàlia Torres in La Seu d'Urgell, Formatgeria La Seu, La Boqueria, La Casa del Bacallà, La Pallaresa, La Vinya del Senyor, the olive oil producers of La Bisbal de Falset, Oriol Balaguer, Pla de Palau, Quimet & Quimet, Restaurant Sant Pau, Salero, Santa Maria, Set Portes, Tèxtil Cafè, Tot Formatge, Vinacoteca, and Xocoa.

PHOTO CREDITS

PHOTOGRAPHY LOCATIONS

The following Barcelona and Catalan locations have been given references for the map on pages 30–31.

PAGE LOCATION (MAP COORDINATES)

PAGE	LOCATION (MAP COORDINATES)
2	La Boqueria market (I6)
4	Museu Nacional d'Art de Catalunya (G5)
6	Escribà bakery, La Rambla (I6)
10	La Boqueria market (I6)
12	El Xampanet tapas bar (J6)
13	Casa Batlló (Gaudí) on passeig de Gracia (I4)
15	Comerç 24 tapas restaurant (J5)
17	La Vinya del Senyor on Plaça de Santa Maria (J6)
19	(upper right) Parc Güell (K1); (lower right) Cal Isidre tapas bar (H6)
21	Born neighbourhood (J6)
27	Parc Güell (K1)
32	Cal Pep tapas bar (J6)
35	(upper) Bar Pinotxo (I6); (lower right) El Xampanet (J6)
63	(upper) Brunells bakery (J6)
67	(upper) Xocoa chocolate shop (J6)
70	Cal Pep tapas bar (J6)
72	(lower left) La Vinya del Senyor (J6); (lower right) Santa Maria restaurant (J5)
73	(upper left) Espai Sucre restaurant (J6)
81	Escribà bakery, La Rambla (I6)
89	El Xampanet tapas bar (J6)
90	La Pallaresa (I6)
92	Parc Güell (K1)
96	Els Pescadors restaurant (M6)
98	(upper left) Museu Nacional d'Art de Catalunya (G5); (upper right) La Boqueria market (I6)
99	La Barceloneta district (J7)
104	Bar del Pi (I6)
115	La Pedrera (Gaudí) off passeig de Gracia (I4)
116	Chef at Abac restaurant (J6)
120	Calçotada fiesta in Tarragona (B2)
128	La Catedral in the Barri Gòtic (J6)
132	Santa Maria tapas restaurant (J5)
134	(upper left) Set Portes restaurant (J6); (upper right) Santa María del Mar church (J6)
135	(upper left) Els Pescadors (M6); Escribà bakery (I6)
137	Set Portes restaurant (J6)
139	La Boqueria market (I6)
148	Bogatell beach (L7)
155	Santa María del Mar church (J6)
164	La Pallaresa (I6)
166	(lower right) Parc Güell (K1)
167	(upper left) Xocoa chocolate shop (J6)
171	La Pallaresa (I6)
172	La Vinya del Senyor (J6)

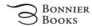
BONNIER
BOOKS

BONNIER BOOKS

Appledram Barns
Birdham Road
Chichester, West Sussex
PO20 7EQ

FOODS OF THE WORLD BARCELONA

Originally published as
Williams-Sonoma Foods of the World Barcelona

Conceived and produced by Weldon Owen Inc.
814 Montgomery Street, San Francisco, CA 94133
Telephone: 415-291-0100 Fax: 415-291-8841

In Collaboration with Williams-Sonoma, Inc.
3250 Van Ness Avenue, San Francisco, CA 94109

A Weldon Owen Production
Copyright © 2006 Weldon Owen Inc.
and Williams-Sonoma, Inc.

All rights reserved, including the right of
reproduction in whole or in part in any form.

Foods of the World is a trademark of Oxmoor House, Inc.

First printed in 2006
10 9 8 7 6 5 4 3 2 1

ISBN 978-1905825-08-0

Printed by Tien Wah Press
Printed in Singapore

WELDON OWEN INC.

Chief Executive Officer John Owen
President and Chief Operating Officer Terry Newell
Vice President International Sales Stuart Laurence
Vice President and Creative Director Gaye Allen
Vice President and Publisher Hannah Rahill
Business Manager Richard Van Oosterhout

Series Editor Kim Goodfriend
Editor Heather Belt
Editorial Assistant Juli Vendzules

Associate Creative Director Leslie Harrington
Art Director Nicky Collings
Designers Nicky Collings, Marisa Kwek
Photo Researcher Liz Lazich
Production Director Chris Hemesath
Colour Specialist Teri Bell
Production and Shipping Coordinator Todd Rechner

Food and Prop Stylist Ana Torróntegui Salazar
Food and Prop Stylist's Assistant Amanda Laporte Breysse
Map Illustrator Scott Panton
Translator Josephine Bacon